Can religion

a public

def. religion

PHILOSOPHERS ON EDUCATION

PHILOSOPHERS ON EDUCATION

Edited by

Roger Straughan

School of Education
University of Reading

and

John Wilson

Department of Educational Studies
University of Oxford

BARNES & NOBLE BOOKS
TOTOWA, NEW JERSEY

First published in the USA 1987 by
BARNES & NOBLE BOOKS
81 ADAMS DRIVE
TOTOWA, NEW JERSEY, 07512

ISBN 0–389–20621–0

Library of Congress Cataloging-in-Publication Data
Philosophers on education.
Includes index.
1. Education—Aims and objectives—Addresses,
essays, lectures. 2. Education—Philosophy—Addresses,
essays, lectures. 3. Moral education—Addresses,
essays, lectures. I. Straughan, Roger. II. Wilson,
John, 1928–
LB41.P574   1987   370'.1   86–3297
ISBN 0–389–20621–0

Contents

v

Acknowledgments

Chapter 3 is reprinted from the *Journal of Philosophy of Education*, vol. 16, No. 2, by permission of the Philosophy of Education Society of Great Britain.

Chapter 10 is reprinted with minor revisions from *Gewirth's Ethical Rationalism: Critical Essays with a Reply by Alan Gewirth*, edited by Edward Regis Jr., (1984) by permission of the University of Chicago Press.

Notes on the Contributors

Renford Bambrough is a Fellow of St John's College, Cambridge, Sidgwick Lecturer in Philosophy, University of Cambridge, and Editor of *Philosophy*. He has held the Stanton Lectureship in the Philosophy of Religion at Cambridge, and visiting appointments at Cornell University, the Universities of California and Oregon and Melbourne University. In 1983 he visited Princeton as a Presidential Fellow of the Carnegie Foundation. He is a member of the Council for the Accreditation of Teacher Education and is the author of *Reason, Truth and God* and *Moral Scepticism and Moral Knowledge*.

Neil Cooper is Professor in Moral Philosophy at the University of Dundee. Educated at the City of London School and Balliol College, Oxford, he has been Senior Scholar, New College, Oxford, John Locke Scholar in Mental Philosophy and Lecturer in Philosophy at the University of St Andrews. He is the author of *The Diversity of Moral Thinking* and of articles on a wide range of philosophical topics.

R. S. Downie is Professor of Moral Philosophy at Glasgow University. He is Chairman of the Working Party of the Central Council for Education and Training in Social Work reporting on the teaching of values in social work courses. He is the author of *Caring and Curing*, *Education and Personal Relationships*, *Roles and Values*, *Respect for Persons*, and *Government Action and Morality*.

Antony Flew is Emeritus Professor of Philosophy at the University of Reading and Distinguished Research Fellow of the Social Philosophy and Policy Centre, Bowling Green, Ohio. He is also a member of the Education Group of the Centre for Policy Studies and the author of *Crime or Disease?*; *Thinking about Thinking*; *Sociology, Equality and Education*; *A Rational Animal*; *The Politics of Procrustes*; *Darwinian Evolution* and of various other books and articles.

R. W. Hepburn is Professor of Moral Philosophy at the University of Edinburgh and has held earlier academic appointments at the Universities of Aberdeen, Nottingham and New York. His publications have been chiefly in the fields of aesthetics, the philosophy of religion and moral philosophy, and include *Christianity and Paradox* and eight shorter studies in *Wonder and Other Essays*.

Martin Hollis is Professor of Philosophy in the School of Economic and Social Studies at the University of East Anglia. He is the author of *Models of Man* and *Invitation to Philosophy*, co-author of *Rational Economic Man* and co-editor of *Rationality and Relativism*. He has published papers in the philosophy of several social sciences.

W. D. Hudson is Reader in Moral Philosophy at the University of Exeter. In 1983–84 he held a research fellowship on the St Luke's College Foundation. Besides university teaching he has done some educational broadcasting to sixth forms and served on advisory committees at the BBC and County Hall. He is the author of *Reason and Right, Modern Moral Philosophy, A Century of Moral Philosophy, A Philosophical Approach to Religion* and *Wittgenstein on Religious Belief*, and has contributed numerous articles to philosophical and theological journals.

Don Locke is Professor of Philosophy at the University of Warwick. He has also taught at the University of Newcastle upon Tyne, the University of Wisconsin-Madison, the American University, Washington, D.C., and the Universities of Auckland, Waikato and Canterbury. He is the author of three books in epistemology and a biography of William Godwin, co-editor of *Morality in the Making*, and has published articles in professional philosophical, psychological and educational journals.

G. H. R. Parkinson is Professor of Philosophy at the University of Reading. He has written on Hegel, on the early philosophy of Wittgenstein and on the theory of meaning, and his books include *Spinoza's Theory of Knowledge, Logic and Reality in Leibniz's Metaphysics* and *Georg Lukács*.

D. Z. Phillips is Professor of Philosophy at the University College of Swansea. He has taught at Queen's College, Dundee, and University College, Bangor, and has been a visiting professor at American and

Canadian universities. Among his books are *The Concept of Prayer*, *Religion without Explanation*, *Through a Darkening Glass*, *Belief*, *Change and Forms of Life* and *R. S. Thomas: Poet of the Hidden God*.

Roger Straughan is Reader in Education at the University of Reading. Prior to taking up this appointment in 1973 he taught in a College of Education and in primary and secondary schools. His main area of research has been the philosophical problems concerning moral education. His publications include *Can We Teach Children to be Good?*; *I Ought to, But ...* and *Philosophizing about Education* (with John Wilson) and several articles on philosophy of education.

John Wilson is a Lecturer and Tutor in the Department of Educational Studies, University of Oxford, and a Fellow of Mansfield College. He has been an Associate Professor of Philosophy of Religion at Trinity College, Toronto; Lecturer in Philosophy in the School of Educational Studies, University of Sussex; and Director of Research with the Farmington Trust Research Unit, Oxford. He is the author of more than thirty books including *What Philosophy Can Do*.

Introduction

In 1973, a high-water mark in the recent history of philosophy of education, Richard Peters, whose herculean efforts over the past twenty years have done more than any other person to put the subject on the map, edited *The Philosophy of Education* in the Oxford Readings in Philosophy series – a clear sign that philosophy of education had finally become respectable in the eyes of pure or proper philosophers. In the introduction to that volume he advocated that philosophy of education should be seen as a branch of philosophy proper and should be in close touch with developments within it, and went on to observe that philosophy of education was at that time suffering from too little fundamental divergence in points of view.[1] A decade later, in a retrospective review of philosophy of education since the 1960s, he concludes by listing what he considers is now needed for the subject's future development: one of the first items to be mentioned is the need for more philosophical depth.[2]

These comments form an interesting background to this collection of articles, all of which are written by philosophers of eminence within various areas of pure philosophy. Despite Peters' call for more divergence in points of view, few attempts have ever been made to encourage such philosophers to write upon educational matters. Yet it must be admitted that the best philosophers, generally speaking and with some honourable exceptions, are not to be found in the area institutionalised under the title philosophy of education. There is certainly much agonising at the moment over the future form and direction which philosophy of education should take and many calls for new approaches and fresh paradigms. In such a situation it seems odd not to enlist the aid of leading figures in the field of philosophy generally, for philosophy of education must surely continue to take note of developments within philosophy itself as well as within education.

The main purpose of this collection, then, is not to comment on or criticise existing work in the philosophy of education as that subject now stands, but to draw upon a distinctively different source for some

1

new perspectives on a variety of educational topics. A further incentive for this enterprise has been an increasing blurring of the distinction between pure and applied philosophy recently and a parallel growth of interest in the application of philosophy to practical issues. The newly formed Society for Applied Philosophy and its associated *Journal of Applied Philosophy* provide but one indication of this trend, while much current work in ethics is now of an applied kind, addressing itself to a wide range of topical moral questions and controversies. The philosophical climate at present, therefore, seems particularly conducive to attempts by philosophers to apply their subject to the business of education.

So what form can this application take? What sort of contribution can philosophers make to educational debate? One important point to emerge from this collection concerns the *diversity* of contribution that is possible. This diversity, which underlines the complex inter-connections between philosophy and education, reveals itself in terms of both content and methodology: there is, in other words, a broad spectrum of educational topics which philosophers can usefully explore, and also a considerable number of different approaches which can be adopted in conducting those explorations. This collec-tion can of course only illustrate this twofold diversity in outline, thus indicating where and how more detailed work still needs to be done. The articles appearing here, then, are in this sense a sample, but (one hopes) a significant sample, and it is thus instructive to review briefly the range of subject matter which this group of philosophers has deemed to be particularly amenable to a philosophic approach and the different approaches which they have used.

Taking the latter point first, at least five levels of philosophising about education are exemplified here. First, the work of a pure philosopher may be analysed and evaluated in such a way as to expose its educational implications; second, the work of educational-ly influential social scientists may be subjected to philosophical scrutiny; third, a topic may be examined which overlaps both philosophy and education; fourth, an educational issue may be tackled directly and shown to raise fundamental philosophical ques-tions; and finally, a philosophical or logical principle may be estab-lished and then applied to certain educational issues and practices. These different approaches are by no means mutually exclusive, and in practice philosophers of education tend to use a mixture of these (and no doubt other) methods, but this collection of articles demons-trates these alternatives particularly clearly. For example, the first approach is illustrated by G. H. R. Parkinson and Renford Bambrough, whose contributions draw upon the work of Rorty and Gewirth respectively; the second by Don Locke, who critically examines some of the work of the psychologist, Lawrence Kohlberg, and its implications for moral education; the third by R. S. Downie and Neil Cooper, who look at ways in which education is connected with knowledge, understanding and independence of mind; the fourth by W. D. Hudson, who asks whether religious education can and should go on in schools; and the fifth by Antony Flew, who applies to a number of topical educational issues the principle that a sincere concern with any purpose presupposes a concern to know whether and how far that purpose has been and is being achieved.

These methodological differences are of considerable interest in themselves. That they are complementary rather than antagonistic to each other, however, is brought out by the shared interests of the contributors in certain fairly specific areas of educational concern.

The articles fall into three main parts, Part I concentrating upon various logical features of educational aims and achievements. D. Z. Phillips argues in Chapter 1 that a number of fallacies are involved in supposing that there can be educational short-cuts which enable intellectual achievements to be arrived at without the travail of intellectual labour; Antony Flew claims in Chapter 2 that any genuinely educational policies must be concerned with what and how much is being learnt, how fast, how well and by how many, and that anyone seriously committed to the pursuit of educational progress must also be committed to the monitoring of all educational achievements and non-achievements; while Martin Hollis in less polemical vein in Chapter 3 examines the extent to which educational goods are positional, in the sense of being valuable to some people only on condition that others do not have them.

Part II explores connections between knowledge and education. Each article looks at different facets of rationality and understanding, and each author makes use of what he sees as a crucial distinction: between bare knowledge and understanding-knowledge in the case of Neil Cooper (Chapter 4), between independence of mind and individuality of mind in the case of R. S. Downie (Chapter 5), and between humanistic education and scientific education in the case of G. H. R. Parkinson (Chapter 6).

Part III focuses more specifically upon the areas of religion and morality. W. D. Hudson in Chapter 7 and R. W. Hepburn in Chapter 8 investigate in different ways the extent to which religion may be said to have a rational basis and as such may be a suitable subject for education; Don Locke in Chapter 9 examines the allegedly rational basis of moral development and moral education, as depicted by Lawrence Kohlberg; while Renford Bambrough in Chapter 10 offers a more general account of the roots of moral reason and of what is involved in becoming initiated into the understanding of good and evil.

There are, then, connections of a fairly obvious kind between the chapters within each section. In addition, the reader will find several recurrent themes emerging throughout the book, such as the nature of understanding and of evidence. More broadly still, it will be found that every chapter in one way or another probes some aspect of reason and rationality and their relationship to the business of education. This common concern is not perhaps too surprising a feature of this collection, given that philosophy has been described as being essentially to do with questions about what is a good reason for what. Nevertheless, the pointers offered by the philosophers who have contributed to this book suggest that philosophy of education still has a unique and vital role to perform in persistently raising those questions in every possible educational context.

NOTES

1. Peters, R. S. (ed.), *The·Philosophy of Education* (Oxford University Press, 1973) pp. 2–4.
2. Peters, R. S., 'Philosophy of Education' in Hirst, P. H. (ed.) *Educational Theory and its Foundation Disciplines* (Routledge, 1983) p. 50.

Part I
The Logic of Educational Aims and Achievements

Part I

1 Education and Magic

D. Z. PHILLIPS

Perhaps I ought to begin with an assurance that this paper is not an attempt to establish or advocate a connection between education and the occult! By 'magic' I mean various attempts to short-circuit intellectual routes by giving the impression that the same achievements can be arrived at without the travail of intellectual labour. Of course, there is no difficulty in imagining such short-cuts being put into operation. They bring about changes in the very conception of education. Yet, this is precisely what advocates of the changes will not admit. On the contrary, it is an essential part of their claim that the *same* intellectual understanding can be attained despite the changes. One has taken a short-cut that is all. The analogy suggested seems to be a simple one. If there are two routes to Swansea, one a long one involving dangers and hardship, and a short one which avoids such dangers and hardships, then who could recommend the long route given that the point of choosing either is to arrive at Swansea as one's destination? Why cannot the same be achieved in education? If there are two routes, one harder than the other, both leading to the same result, why choose the harder one? My contention, however, is that it is impossible to achieve the same result while ignoring the harder way. It is not an experimental issue. There is an internal relation between hard intellectual labour and intellectual understanding. In other words, there is conceptual confusion involved in the suggestion that understanding is contingently related to the means by which it is achieved. When someone says that the same can be achieved by the short-cut he is deluding himself. Yet, all these conclusions, dogmatically stated like this at the outset, must be argued for.

Perhaps I can illustrate at the outset what I mean by reference to Marlowe's and Goethe's treatment of the Faust legend.[1] If most people were asked to say what they know of the Faust legend, no doubt they would refer to Faust's pact with the Devil, and to his desire to make secure a woman's love. In return for his soul he wants the Devil to make the woman love him. His impatience is obvious:

'Spare me, Professor Plausible, your saws
And plaguey discourse on the moral laws.
To cut the story short, I tell you plain,
Unless her sweet young loveliness has lain
Within my arms' embrace this very night,
The stroke of twelve shall end our pact outright.'

Yet, if this is what he wants, 'to cut the story short', we must remember that he wants it as much in the realm of learning as in relation to the woman he wants to possess. He wants to rank with the gods, to know everything all at once. The arduousness of the intellectual journey has begun to irritate him. Thus we find Geothe's Faust saying,

'... Too well I feel
My kinship with the worm, who loves the soil,
Who feeds on dust until the wanderer's heel
Gives sepulture to all his care and toil.

Is it not dust, that fills my hundred shelves,
And walls me in like any pedant hack?
Fellow of moth that flits and worm that delves,
I drag my life through learned bric-a-brac.
And shall I here discover what I lack,
And learn, by reading countless volumes through,
That mortals mostly live on misery's rack,
That happiness is known to just a few?'

Marlowe's Faustus speaks in a similar vein:

'Is 'to dispute well logic's chiefest end'?
Affords this art no greater miracle?
Then read no more: thou hast attained that end.'

What Faust is searching for here cannot be attained. There is no way in which the intellectual conclusion can be appreciated in isolation from the arguments that sustain it. Of course, I am not claiming that conclusions or assumptions cannot be taken at face value, but when this happens on a wide scale it leads to intellectual mediocrity, a dead jargon unsupported by any critical life. Teaching those coming to philosophy for the first time illustrates this point. If one fails to awaken any philosophical puzzlement, the student will desperately try to commit to memory certain philosophical theses. Yet, these theses might just as well express their contradictories as far as the non-puzzled student is concerned, since the theses are not, for him, the product of an intellectual struggle.

It is interesting to find that as disillusionment with enquiry sets in, what Faust longs for is control, the ability to do things. It is in these terms that Marlowe's Faustus is tempted by the Evil Angel:

'Go forward, Faustus, in that famous art
Wherein all nature's treasure is contained.
Be thou on earth as Jove is in the sky,
Lord and commander of these elements.'

The prospect of such control dazzles him:

'How am I glutted with conceit of this!
Shall I make spirits fetch me what I please,
Resolve me of all ambiguities,
Perform what desperate enterprise I will?'

Enquiry is something which must sustain *him*. It must give *him* control. And, yet, going back to his desire to make a woman's love secure through the Devil's pact, we find that he comes to realise that what he wants cannot be found in this way. However natural Margareta's response seems to be, he can never be sure of its reality because of what surrounds it and gives it its meaning. It lacks the surroundings of natural development being the product of the Devil's work. When natural love for Margareta does develop in Faust, therefore, it is little wonder that we find a conflict arising within him born of the naturalness of his love and the unnaturalness of the context in which it has to operate. So although the Devil keeps his promise and brings him to Margareta's room he finds that things are not as he had wanted them to be:

'And you, good Sir; your purpose here, your quest?
How moved and troubled is my cloudy breast!

What make you here? Why is your heart so sore?
Ah, wretched Faust, I know you now no more!
I thought to follow hot on passion's flair,
And now I languish for a true-love's bliss.'

There is a tension between the prominence he has wanted to give to the satisfaction of his own desires – to which Margareta should be the support – and the fact that he finds himself absorbed in her with no thought of his prior plans.

Similar tensions, despite obvious differences, can be found in the realm of intellectual enquiry. Here again there would be a tension between a desire to make enquiry a supporting activity, a sustaining of the self, and absorption in the characteristic problems of the enquiry in question. A man who gives himself to enquiry does not make enquiry an end or see himself as *the* agent of enquiry. This truth has been given forceful expression by John Anderson. He speaks of 'the ridiculous overworking of the conception of support':

Prior speaks of things that we ... support; but what are 'we'? Pure individuals, extensionless centres of force to which various pursuits become somehow attached? If it were true that we support inquiry and the rest, it would be some specific activity in us (perhaps, the inquiring activity itself) that did the supporting. But does inquiry, or does any other activity, pursue inquiry as an objective? ... Now it is undeniable that inquirers can learn to expect the extension of inquiry under certain conditions, also that in the course of these communications certain 'rules' (things to be remembered, things to be avoided, etc.) come to be formulated and, further, that the existence and modes of operation of forces hostile to inquiry come to be recognised. But it is still inquiring that is the agent in all this, and, if it forms a policy, it is not itself the *object* of that policy; and, in particular, it will be weakened unless it sits loosely to its rules and, for the most part, forgets about them. This, I think, will be admitted by many with regard to education, and it should not be hard for these people to admit it with regard to cultural communication in general.[2]

As we saw, however, Faust does want to stand as *the* agent to enquiry and wants that enquiry to support him. That is partly why we see a degeneration in his conception of education from understanding to a desire for control. Inevitably, given such degeneration, estrangement from intellectual enquiry results with the hope that magic will provide the short-cut. Magic, it is hoped, replaces absorption in enquiry with instant understanding as a means of control. Thus Marlowe's Faustus reaches his conclusion:

> Philosophy is odious and obscure.
> Both law and physic are for petty wits.
> Divinity is basest of the three,
> Unpleasant, harsh, contemptible and vile.
> 'Tis magic, magic that hath revished me.

Yet, just as magic could not determine for him a love freely given, so magic cannot give him the understanding he seeks for. This is not because magic is ineffective where something else might do the trick, but because there is a confusion in the very conception of what is sought. Faust looks for instant understanding, as if it were some kind of isolatable occurrence which could be given to him. Many philosophers have asked, 'What *is* understanding?' as if one could single out the occurrence from all the characteristic things a man does and the characteristic things that can be expected of him when he is said to understand. In this context Wittgenstein asks us to consider the following example:

> A writes a series of numbers down; B watches him and tries to find a law for the sequence of numbers. If he succeeds he exclaims: Now I can go on!' – So this capacity, this understanding, is something that makes its appearance in a moment. So let us try and see what it is that makes its appearance here. – A has written down the numbers 1, 5, 11, 19, 29; at this point B says he knows how to go on. What happened here? Various things may have happened; for example, while A was slowly putting one number after another, B was occupied with trying various algebraic formulae on the numbers which had been written down. After A had written the number 19 B tried the formula $A_n = n^2 + n - 1$; and the next number confirmed his hypothesis.
>
> Or again, B does not think of formulae. He watches A writing his numbers down with a certain feeling of tension, and all sorts of vague thoughts go through his head. Finally he asks himself: 'What is the series of differences?' He finds the series 4, 6, 8, 10 and says: Now I can go on.

Or he watches and says 'Yes I know *that* series' – and continues it, just as he would have done if A had written down the series 1, 3, 5, 7, 9. – Or he says nothing at all and simply continues the series. Perhaps he had what may be called the sensation 'that's easy!' (Such a sensation is, for example, that of a light quick intake of breath, as when one is mildly startled.)[3]

Commenting on this example Norman Malcolm says,

Now if we ask *what* the sudden understanding was, it is evident that the answer is not that it consisted in B's thinking of the formula: 'For it is perfectly imaginable that the formula should occur to him and that he should nevertheless not understand.'[4] One could pronounce, or see in one's mind, a certain formula without knowing how to use it. Nor can the answer be that B's sudden understanding consisted in his thinking of the next numbers in the sequence, nor in his writing them down for someone might accidentally get the first few numbers right but fail to understand the series. Nor can it consist in the sudden relief of tension. And so on. We see that none of these phenomena, which Wittgenstein calls 'characteristic *accompaniments*' of sudden understanding, *is* the understanding. We cannot put our finger on *anything* occurring at the moment of understanding, which *is* the understanding. *The understanding itself is not anything we can single out or fix our attention on.*

This technique of 'dissolving' various mental processes and occurrences does not prove that there is no such thing as sudden deciding, or understanding or remembering. Obviously there is nothing wrong with saying that someone suddenly remembered where he put his keys. What is proved is that there is not, in addition to the characteristic accompaniments, another occurrence which is the remembering itself, and on which one's attention can dwell.[5]

But this is precisely what Faust seeks and what cannot be attained: understanding without its characteristic accompaniments. Not even magic can produce what is logically impossible. These conclusions about understanding throw light on a number of areas in education. Let us consider some examples.

First, our conclusions can be seen to throw light on the nature of emotions and moral reactions, an understanding of which plays a central part in certain aspects of literary criticism.

In an effort to discover the essence of human emotion, an attempt may be made to isolate it as a phenomenon from its characteristic accompaniments. When this is attempted there will be a tendency to talk of moral reactions or emotions as if they were sensations. If we can feel pain for a second, why not remorse? But nothing so felt could be remorse, since we would not say that a person had felt remorse unless his attitude towards what he has done has implications for his future conduct. Anything lasting a second would lack the dispositional seriousness which remorse must have. To think otherwise is linked to the misunderstandings found in certain forms of sentimentality and romanticism. Consider the following example. A man may claim to show compassion because he 'gulps with emotion' when confronted with certain situations. Yet he shows no pity or compassion to those around him. When he is accused of lacking these moral reactions, he claims that he is deeply moved by human distress. What are we to make of this claim? Is it his physical reaction, his gulping, which is to determine his moral reactions, or is it his moral attitude which determines the weight we should give to the physical reaction? From what we have seen, the latter alternative is the correct one. It helps us to locate one characteristic of romanticism and sentimentality in their tendency to divorce discrete sensations from behavioural dispositions. Think of someone who thinks that the firmness of a friendship is like the firmness of a handshake. It would be foolish to rely on such a man! He would think that the firmness of a friendship, through good times and bad, could be made secure as easily as the increase of pressure in a handshake. When one partner may tell another that their marriage or relationship is over, the rejected partner may cling to the other in desperation, as if clinging to the body could somehow cling on to the relationship as well. It is as if the enfolding embrace could create a haven within which the relationship would be safe. This is precisely what the embrace is allowed to do in romantic novellas. Despite untold troubles, peace is found within embracing arms. No matter how complex the difficulties, characters are made to look into each other's eyes and, suddenly, they know all will be well. The novellas are cheap and romantic precisely because the authors make no effort to show how the embrace and the look are related to the troubles and complexities to which we have been introduced. The look or the embrace are simply supposed to work without any mediation of any kind. The characters simply 'know' that they are safe, or that all will be well, despite the fact that such knowledge has no justification or location in what we have seen of them or their situations. The stability or knowledge, cut off from their characteristic accompaniments, thus become the empty products of the romantic and sentimental mentality.

Second, let us examine how the philosophical insights we have noted could save us from squandering energy on educational enquiries which are rooted in conceptual confusion. Let us take an example from religious studies during the period when the notion of alternative cultures was prominent, a period in which popular experimentation with drugs played a major part. Here, too, efforts were made to locate the essence of religious experience, to locate some sensory experience which could be isolated from its surroundings. Claims were made for drug-taking as a method for short-cutting the route to religious experience. There was much discussion, for example, about the possibility of instant mysticism. This, indeed, would be an incredible achievement, if possible. After all, the summit of mystical experience for many mystics, mystical union, is believed to be possible only within the context of a highly developed spirituality. Many a mother superior has had to tell a young novice, as charitably as possible, that her claim to have attained mystical union is rather premature. Yet now it was said that simply through taking drugs instant mystical experience could be attained. Drugs could open up a world of experience never dreamt of before, it was claimed. No one denies that drugs will affect perception and other experience in many ways. The point remains, however, that the significance of any sensory changes will depend on their relation to the rest of a person's life. It is this relation, how the sensory experience is taken up into a person's life, which determines whether that experience is to have a significant or a banal aspect. The suggestion, therefore, that an intake of drugs could, of itself, causally guarantee a mystical experience is simply a conceptual confusion masquerading as an empirical hypothesis.

It was depressing at the time to see how much so-called intellectual respectability was attributed to these claims. I remember one occasion on which a group of reporters and investigators hovered over a delightful young lady who had claimed that drugs had given her an unprecedented insight into the nature of reality. They now awaited the details of the revelation, the drugs having been taken. The lady had been playing with an orange when she made her claim. The details of the nature of reality when they finally came through were hardly surprising. 'It's all orange', she said! Is it not clear that it is the beliefs, attitudes, values, etc. which take up and given significance to the sensory experiences involved and not vice versa?

Third, consider another attempt to cut the story short, this time in relation to the sciences. The claim is often made that certain sciences are young sciences, and that big questions, insoluble at the moment, will be resolved one day. It is not that such claims are inherently confused. Obviously, they are not. The point is that sometimes they are confused. The example I have in mind is such a case. Substantial grants are given to scientists to investigate aggression in animals. I do not want to comment on their findings one way or another. What I do want to note is the distant hope, often connected with these investigations, namely, that learning about animal aggression may well hold the key to human aggression. Again, I want to say that here we have conceptual confusions in the guise of empirical enquiry. One cannot get very far in explaining human aggression without invoking the ideas, tensions, etc., involved in the situations in which the aggression occurs. Yet, these tensions and ideas have no part in the life of animals. It has been said that studying aggression in rats may lead, one day, to the prevention of wars between human beings. The complex analysis of how a particular war occurs, involving as it may well, economic, political, religious, military and other considerations, can in no way be reduced to studies of animal aggression. How can a level of explanation which contains no reference to the various aspects of human life which go up to make a war, be said to contain the essence of those various aspects? What we can conclude in this context, as in previous ones, is that there can be no short-cut in the investigations, no by-passing of the complex aspects of human history.

Fourth, we can see how spurious short-cuts may be sought in education itself. We find attempts to isolate the phenomenon of learning. Here, too, it has been thought that studying the behaviour of animals will yield the essence we are searching for. Is not our task that of determining the stimulus which will lead men to learn? It was thought that the behaviour of hungry rats who could be taught at the sound of a bell to go through a certain door which had food behind it, could throw light on learning in education. The conclusion seemed to follow naturally from the facts: behaviour can be appropriately modified given a correspondingly appropriate stimulus. That stimulus takes the form of an incentive. Thus, in relation to education, we have a stimulus–response theory which distorts what we already know. The response required is the learning, and the stimulus which will bring this about is some form or other of incentive. I said that this distorts what we already know. Our task is not to challenge the empirical results of experiments concerning the rat, with empirical results of some other kind. On the contrary, all we need do is to remind ourselves that learning comes about when a person gives himself to the discipline in question. What it is to have learning is internally related to involvement in the subject. If, on the other hand, one places the point of learning in the incentive, a relocation of the incentive will be sufficient, in itself, to render pointless that which once had a point. In this way, all serious discussion about the curriculum is by-passed. A serious discussion would have to consider whether a refusal or readiness to change the curriculum in any respect led to a gain or loss in intellectual understanding. A non-serious discussion would simply be a political matter, influencing the various aspects of the curriculum simply by strengthening or weakening the various incentives connected with them. The price of such a short-cut would be no less than a by-passing of the discussion of the very content of an educational curriculum. If you think of discussions which surround educational policies, ask yourselves how many of them actually concern mattes of the intellect, and how many of them concern matters which, no matter how important they may be to various people for other reasons, show little concern for intellectual questions.

What we have seen in this chapter, beginning with Faust, and in the four examples we have considered, is that the story cannot be cut short and remain the same story. When Faust asked for instant understanding, he was asking for something which is conceptually impossible. He could not arrive at understanding and also by-pass the intellectual routes by which it is reached. Since understanding is not something apart from its characteristic accompaniments in the lives of men, the patterns of behaviour in which it has its life, to search for understanding in isolation from accompaniments and patterns is to search for something which does not exist.

Having reached this conclusion, it must be admitted that not all human beings display the characteristic patterns of understanding in matters of the intellect. Some have suggested that there are reasons for this. Reasons of different kinds and emphases have been offered, some making inherited genetic differences central, and others making social differences of wealth and education into which a child is born central. It is not my concern now to question these explanations. Taking the differences as given, I want to illustrate how magic may intervene again in our reactions to them. The two reactions I want to discuss attempt to correct the differences by cutting the story short, so that despite the different starting-points, somehow or other, the same end result can be attained. If, however, as I have argued, the short-cut is conceptually impossible, the alleged equality achieved must be an illusion.

The first reaction in academic life I want to consider concerns entrance into universities. It is an undeniable fact that children are born into homes where the availability of educational facilities varies enormously. Some children may never see a book. This being so, is it not unfair to give them the same assessment for acceptance into universities? We should encourage lower entry requirements for those who have been educationally deprived. Yet, it would be foolish to think that this in itself solves the problem. Why should one think that the short years of a university course can compensate for the long years of deprivation which precede it? Therefore, the background of the student should be kept in mind throughout his career and especially in the assessment of his degree. But, of course, none of this can give what it claims to give. An essential part of the promise is that you, if you have been deprived, will be given the same as the others have. Yet, this is impossible if, in fact, there has been the kind of compensation I have mentioned. Let us suppose a man has had an upper-second class degree. Of course, if all he concerns himself with is the label and what it will get him, all is (prudentially) well. But more is needed psychologically for self-respect. A man needs to tell himself that he does deserve the degree he has, not in the sense that someone else has thought him to be a deserving compensatory case, but as someone who has attained the academic standard associated with the degree. Yet, if he knows that he is a compensatory case, this cannot work. The very fact of compensation means that he did not attain that standard. On the other hand, if he is not told, he becomes the unwary victim of condescension. 'Condescension' is not too strong a word here. One has only to imagine a man who does care about the standard he has attained reacting to the news that his degree does not in fact correspond to the standard he actually attained. Let us suppose that a man attains first-class honours in philosophy. He is then told, 'Of course, you realise that the first-class honours degree we have given you is the kind we give to the sons of Welsh miners. There is another kind we give to bank-managers' sons and yet another kind for the products of public schools.' Would he not be justified in telling them what to do with their so-called first-class honours degree? And if they do not tell him what is happening isn't that even worse? By contrast with all this, I heard of a product of the University of Oregon who, despite being unemployed, refuses to accept a university teaching post in philosophy which he could have in a quota system for employing members of ethnic minorities. He wants to be appointed as a philosopher, and not as anything else. This is a man who does not confuse condescension and concern, and who knows that magic cannot eliminate the difference.

The second reaction in academic life I want to consider concerns the possibility that when intellectual competence is challenged by some form of examination, failure may be the result. There are those who would like to eliminate that possibility. For them, to say that a person has failed to reach an academic standard is to create an unnecessary elitism. Furthermore, it is to treat a human being in a way in which no human being should be treated – it is to say that he is a failure as a person. Is this true? Why should telling a man that he has failed to reach a required standard imply that he is worthless as a person? Intellectual pursuits do not make up the whole of life, so why should it not be possible to convey judgements concerning them without any such implication? It may be said that this is impossible because of a pervasive social snobbishness which does look on so many other pursuits as inferior. Even so, however, it may well be asked whether this justifies distorting intellectual judgements. It may even be the case that those who want to protect people from such judgements are themselves the victims of the very elitism they pride themselves on avoiding. The reason why they do not say a man has failed to reach an academic standard is because they *do* believe he can be written off as a person if we say so. Yet, in the end, these social or personal deficiencies should not be our yardstick if we are concerned with academic judgements. Why should these lead us to adopt protectionist attitudes? Protectionism entails a distinction between protectors and protected. The protectors are those who will still know the realities of a man's academic attainments, and the protected are those who they think are not up to hearing the news of their deficiencies. To criticise a work, even to say it is deplorable is, in one sense, a compliment. The standard of the work may not be complimented, but the person criticised is at least treated as someone who is worthy of honest comment. He is not treated therapeutically as someone not up to hearing the news. Of course, even if the language of failure is not used, all the intellectual consequences will remain unchanged. These will be discovered in practice in different and, probably, less savoury ways.[6] The attempt at cutting the story short, magic, not only cannot achieve what it pretends to achieve,' it also creates new evils.

This last conclusion may seem hard to grasp. I have called the various reactions I have discussed magic, and said that they are riddled with conceptual confusions. This being so, it may give the impression that whether we detect them or not has no practical consequences. After all, are we not dealing with logical impossibilities? This reaction would be a mistake. True, these reactions cannot be what they claim to be, for that is indeed conceptually confused. Nevertheless, people do act on their confused beliefs and confused practices result. Confused practices are nevertheless practices, and the realm of education has more than enough of them. In the examples I considered, confusion may, and does, often win the day. Romanticism may dominate human relationships and with it a correspondingly appropriate view of the emotions as transient sensations. A language may, or rather has, developed which reflects these influences. Thus persons or interests become talked of as things which may 'turn us on' or 'turn us off'. Education may become permeated with requests for short-cuts. The language of excellence may be replaced by one of quotas and proportions, and the language of disinterestedness by one of incentives.

Yet, if all this happens, why call it confusion? Why not say that we now simply have different conceptions of morality, religion, human relationships and education? The reason for speaking of confusion is that the new conceptions want to travel in the name of the old. If they were clear about what they were doing, one might not like it, one might oppose it, but there would be no confusion involved. But when they think they are doing what they are not, there confusion of concepts unites with confusion of practice.

Let us end as we began with Faust. Faust wants to summon up the Devil and imagines all the horrifying ways in which he may appear. He also wonders by what route the Devil is able to visit him from his distant awesome abode in Hell. Yet, when Mephistophilis appears to Marlowe's Faustus, Faustus comes to realise that hell is not the distant place of occult thought. He asks Mephistophilis, 'How comes it then that thou art out of hell?' The reply is unhesitating 'Why, this is hell, nor am I out of it'. Goethe's Faust anticipates the Devil's coming in some dreadful form, but in walks a fellow academic:

So, that is then the essence of the brute!
A travelling scholar? Time for laughter yet!

Of course, it is not time for laughter, since the demonic realises itself in the mode of Faust's own profession. What can be said of the demonic can be said of confusion. No doubt educational institutions may and have come about where what I have called confusions are in the ascendancy. But no matter how attractive the surface appearance or traditional the trappings, before we congratulate them, we had better look rather closely at that begowned figure in charge of the proceedings.

NOTES

1. For a fuller discussion of this treatment in relation to philosophical discussions of divine foreknowledge see my paper, 'Knowledge, Patience and Faust', *The Yale Review* (forthcoming).
2. John Anderson, 'Ethics and Advocacy' in *Studies in Empirical Philosophy* (Angus & Robertson, 1962) pp. 285–6.
3. Ludwig Wittgenstein, *Philosophical Investigations*, §151.
4. Ibid., §152.
5. Norman Malcolm, *Problems of Mind* (Allen & Unwin, 1972) pp. 33–4.
6. These comments on 'failure' appeared in a slightly different form as 'We Need a Concept Of Failure', *Times Higher Educational Supplement*, 10 Sept. 1976.

2 Examination not Attempted

ANTONY FLEW

'The unexamined life is not to be endured'

Socrates

I

David Hume, at the beginning of Part I of Section IV of his first *Enquiry*, makes much of a distinction between two quite fundamentally different sorts of what we should now call propositions. He asserts: 'All the objects of human reason or enquiry may naturally be divided into two kinds, to wit, *Relations of Ideas*, and *Matters of Fact*.[1]' In making such a distinction Hume did of course have predecessors. For instance, in the *Monadology* Leibniz says:

> There are also two kinds of *truths*, those of *reasoning* and those of *fact*. Truths of reasoning are necessary and their opposite is impossible, and those of fact are contingent and their opposite is possible. When a truth is necessary its reason can be found by analysis, resolving it into more simple ideas and truths until we reach those which are primitive (S. 33).

What is new in Hume is not the drawing of the distinction but the use which he makes of it. It is in this aggressive employment that it has been aptly nicknamed Hume's Fork. By wielding that weapon he is able to conclude that whole *Enquiry* with a peroratory purple paragraph. This has since adorned many a lesser, drabber essay:

> When we run over libraries, persuaded of these principles, what havoc must we make? If we take in our hand any volume; of

21

divinity of school metaphysics, for instance; let us ask, *Does it contain any abstract reasoning concerning quantity or number?* No. *Does it contain any experimental reasoning concerning matter of fact and existence?* No. Commit it then to the flames: for it can contain nothing but sophistry and illusion.

The starting point of the present chapter is just as simple, just as fundamental, and just as *a priori*. The difference is that here we have not the drawing of a distinction but the vindication of a truth. That truth established, the main task becomes to realize some of the possibilities for wreaking havoc. The havoc to be wrought, however, will all be havoc among various hypocrisies, misdirections, false assumptions and other similar obstacles obstructing efforts to get the best and the most possible educational output out of whatever resource input may be from time to time available. The hope is that the appreciation of one simple and, once understood, scarcely deniable point will raise and maintain what has been well characterized, in another context, as a gale of creative destruction.[2]

II

Years ago I applied what is now to be an entirely general contention to the particular case of 'Teaching and Testing'.[3] The crux then was that you cannot truly be said to be sincerely trying to teach – or, for that matter, to learn – unless you are constantly alert to discover how far the material proposed for teaching, or learning, actually is being mastered.[4] It is, therefore, one thing to reject some particular method of testing and assessment, or some particular practice in the employment of the findings thereof. It is quite another to repudiate all testing and assessment in general and as such. When, as has in these last years sometimes happened, professing teachers or professing students commit themselves to such wholesale repudiations, then these manifestos ought to be construed, and forthwith accepted, as acts of resignation from whatever status and emoluments such 'teachers' and 'students' were previously enjoying within the educational world – within, as Tom Lehrer would put it in his often aptly salutary and astringent put-down, Edbiz.

Again it will not do, notwithstanding that it is all too frequently done, to proceed with ranting polemic confidence: from the truistic premise that there are forms of educational attainment which it is not sensible to try to measure through the mechanism of three-hour written examinations; to the illicit and necessarily false conclusion that there are forms which cannot be in any way measured or identified at all. Certainly it would be silly to assess the success or failure of a programme of moral education by discovering how well or ill the class was able to regurgitate approved moral maxims. It would, nevertheless, be even more absurd not to ask whether there had been any resultant improvement in the conduct of pupils exposed to that programme; whether, for instance, there had been any consequent declines in the incidence of theft or of bullying or of vandalism.

So, if professing teachers are so imprudent as to claim that what they are themselves striving to put across is too elusive and too etherial to be captured by tests or measures of any kind whatever, then they should be told – kindly but very, very firmly – to find something else to teach, something teachable. For thus to pretend to be teaching something the learning or not learning of which is indiscernible is as grotesque as *The Hunting of the Snark*. What sense does it make to pretend to pursue quarry which, as the supposed hunters themselves maintain, could not be identified even if it were to be caught?

The point here, however, is not limited to the more particular case of teaching and testing. It is not only, that is, that no one can be truly said to be sincerely trying to teach save in so far as they are constantly concerned to monitor the success or failure of their attempts; as well as being resolved and ready to change their tactics if ever and whenever those previously employed turn out to have been ineffective. Instead it is now maintained that we have here a completely general and highly explosive truth. For sincerity in any purpose whatsoever absolutely presupposes a strong concern to know whether and how far that cherished purpose has been or is being achieved. Furthermore, if and in so far as it is known that it has not been or is not being achieved, we cannot, unless the agent is prepared to adopt alternative tactics, truly say that that same purpose continues to be sincerely and rationally harboured. This general truth, along with all its particular instantiations, is a truth about the relations of ideas rather than about matters of fact. For it is not Descartes only, but all the rest of us also, who preferred, or prefer, to discover the actual intentions and the sincere beliefs both of other people, and even of ourselves, by looking to what is done, or not done, rather than to what – with whatever appearances of impeccable integrity – is merely said.

Suppose, for example, that someone proclaims a Quest for the Holy Grail. Suppose that, almost as soon as the fanfares have died, he settles for the first antique-seeming mug offered by the first fluent rogue in the local bazaar. Then we surely have to say that his neglect of any serious and systematic inquiry, his total lack of interest in either the history of the purchase put in the place of honour on his mantelpiece or the evidence that the real thing does after all survive somewhere, conspire together to show that, whatever else he may have been after, he most certainly was not sincerely trying to unearth and acquire the vessel actually used in the original Last Supper. Again – to take two less elevated illustrations – suppose that someone professes to be in business in order, no doubt among other things, to make a profit; or to be playing cricket in order, again no doubt among other things, to win the match. Then what credence can we give to such professions if we find that he is just not interested in the accounts; or that he is indifferent as to whether or not anyone is keeping the score?

III

The next step, in Section III, is to relate the logical linkages displayed in Section II to the main methodological recommendations of Sir Karl Popper. He has proposals, which are of course closely connected with one another, for the spheres both of science and of social policy. In each case Popperian methodology can be seen as the direct outcome of sincerity in the appropriate purpose. It is the more worthwhile to present these fundamental Popperian recommendations in this way in as much as he himself seems never to have spelt out any such implications. His apparent reluctance to do so, and the consequent failure to deploy what is perhaps the most powerful argument for his own methodology, are probably to be explained by reference to his wholly honourable unwillingness to attribute, or even to recognise, in any of his intellectual opponents, either academic bad faith or any other discreditable distractions. It is an unwillingness shared, like so much else, with his lifelong friend Friedrich Hayek.

(i) The aim in science is truth. Given this aim then the critical approach must follow. The person who truly wants the truth, like the knight who with pure heart and single mind seeks the Holy Grail, cannot embrace unexamined candidates. He must be ever ready to test, and test, and test again. Popper of course goes on to make further claims, some of which are far more disputatious: 'Science', he tells us, 'is not a system of certain ... statements; nor is it a system which steadily advances towards a state of finality. Our science is not knowledge (epistēmē): it can never claim to have attained truth ...' .[5] Whatever we may think of these additions, and especially of that final confession of incurable scepticism, we have to allow that insistence upon a restlessly critical approach is a mark – indeed the mark – of the sincerity of our desire for truth herself; and of our refusal to be content with any substitute – however plausible, seductive, comfortable, congenial or otherwise appealing that substitute might be.

(ii) Parallel considerations apply to the advancement of social policies. If you want to claim that it is to secure some relief of man's estate that you are pushing this policy, then you must be on guard to monitor its success or failure by that standard. You would indeed be best advised to build provisions for such monitoring into every programme you propose. For how can you pretend, for instance, that it is in order to cure the curiously elusive yet apparently pervasive ills of alienation that a Marxist–Leninist revolution is needed; when you never think to try to construct an alienation index; nor to ask what is found when such an index is applied to various groups within various different social systems; nor yet to reflect on the reasons why the workings of your own most favoured regimes are so largely closed to independent investigation?

Popper's advocacy of piecemeal and reformist social engineering – as against its wholesale, revolutionary, and Utopian opposite – should be recognised as the consequence and expression of his sincere and rational commitment to the welfare of the beneficiaries, or victims. For Popper's crucial objection to Utopian social engineering precisely is that it must make the monitoring of success, and the cybernetic correction of failure, impossible. Thus, he says:

> the reconstruction of society is a big undertaking which must cause considerable inconvenience to many and for a considerable span of time. Accordingly, the Utopian engineer will have to be deaf to many complaints: in fact it will be part of his business to suppress unreasonable objections. [He will say, like Lenin, 'You can't make an omelette without breaking eggs.'] But with it, he must invariably suppress reasonable criticism also'.[6]

Other difficulties arise from the length of the Utopian time-scale.

Especially in a period when one of the two British parties of government regularly boasts in its electoral proclamations a sinister determination to enforce 'irreversible changes', and when more of

our academics than ever before claim the Marxist name, there can be
no better ending to the present Section III than a manifesto of
Popperian politics, with its cooling card for the trumpeted pretensions of 'scientific socialism'. The piecemeal method, he suggests,

> might lead to the happy situation where politicians begin to look
> out for their own mistakes instead of trying ... to prove that they
> have always been right. This – and not Utopian planning or
> historical prophecy – would mean the introduction of scientific
> method into politics, since the whole secret of scientific method is
> a readiness to learn from mistakes.[7]

IV

It is high time, and overtime, to begin wreaking some of that
promised havoc. Yet one essential preliminary has still to be com-
pleted. That is to underline two additional truisms, both widely
neglected if never perhaps outright denied: first, that what education
is all about is teaching and learning; and, second, that all teaching
must itself be altogether subordinate to learning – in the sense that
teaching has to be justified by reference not to the efforts or the
intentions or the qualifications of the teachers, but rather to resulting
eductional achievement or non-achievement in the taught.

Any genuinely educational policies must, therefore, be concerned
with what and how much is being learnt, how fast, how well, and by
how many. Genuinely educational policies, here and later, are thus
being contrasted with all those so-called 'policies for education',
which are in fact directed primarily or even exclusively at ends not
essentially connected with learning; or, at any rate, not with acquiring particular skills or mastering particular subjects. The further
consequence which we can now draw is that anyone sincerely
committed to the pursuit of educational progress must be correspondingly committed to the monitoring of all actual educational achievements, and non-achievements.

(i) When, however, 'persuaded of these principles' we start to
survey our public educational system, and to attend to debates about
the future development of that system, we cannot but be both
astonished and appalled: not only by the incompleteness and the
other inadequacies of the monitoring; but also by the failure in those
debates to take account of the findings of what monitoring there is.

Take as a first, breathtaking example the statements made in a review of the record of the 1964–70 labour administration by one of the most academically able of recent Ministers: 'expenditure in education rose from 4.8% of GNP in 1964 to 6.1% in 1970. As a result, all classes of the community enjoyed significantly more education than before'. The second of these propositions is thus asserted as an immediate inference from the first. The only further reason offered for believing that conclusion is that 'The huge expansion in the supply of teachers produced a steady reduction in the pupil/teacher ratio.'[8]

These ministerial arguments will, of course, go through only given two assumptions. Yet neither assumption could be known to true, even if they were true, without attending both to education output – that is to say, achieved learning – and to the relations and lack of relations between such output and various forms of resource input. The first and more unbelievable is that in this peculiarly privileged field expenditure is always cost-effective. That, it should go without saying, is known to be false.[9] But to discuss whether it is or is not false is not to us now relevant. What is both relevant and important is that so many of those who appear to be making the present assumption are not interested in, or are even hostile to, those output-oriented investigations which are essential to the sensible settling of any questions of this kind.

The second necessary assumption is that within the relevant range – between, say, 45 and 15 – smaller classes produce better results. Even if we knew that this was true, and equally true for all subjects and at all levels, anyone sincerely and rationally dedicated to obtaining the best possible results from whatever resources are from time to time available would still want to press the question with which Yeats is said to have responded to the news of his Nobel Prize: 'How much?' For, unless the consequent improvements in learning results are very large, such a person will have to consider possible alternative ways to get more output at the same cost. Teacher's salaries are, after all, by far the biggest item in every education budget. Again, however, it is none of our business here to discover the true answers to such first-order questions.

What is both relevant and important is to draw attention to both the fact and the significance of the fact that the DES under several successive Ministers, as well as the whole national and local Edbiz establishment, have been pressing on with a policy of indiscriminately 'improving' pupil/teacher ratios, without having any decisive evidence that this is the best method, or even one method, of getting better learning results; and without even calling for or commissioning the research which might definitively settle disputes.[10] How can we interpret this fact save as an index, either of a scandalous indifference to the proper objectives of any genuinely educational policy, or of an equally scandalous political irrationality?

(ii) But these faults are not the faults of professional politicians only, nor of professional politicians of only one party. Consider, for instance, a typical House of Commons debate under the heading 'Education'. In 1981 the Opposition motion, introduced by Mr Neil Kinnock, simply took it for granted that the relations between input and output are here direct, constant and uniform: 'That this House', it began, 'recognising the direct relationship between the mainte-nance and enhancement of educational standards and an appropriate investment of resources ...'; and so it went on, and on and on.

The Ministerial amendment moved by Mr Mark Carlisle did at least mention value for money. It expressed "confidence in the ability of the education service ... to secure maximum educational value from the extensive resources which continue to be available to it'. Yet in the rest of his speech the Minister made no attempt to justify such confidence. Like so many of his predecessors in similar debates he could think only of offering formidable figures of increasing expendi-ture:

> Some 5.5% of the gross national product of this country, or twice what it was in 1950, today goes on education. ... In 1979–80 more was spent on the schools in real terms than ever before, twice as much in total and half as much again per pupil as 20 years ago. Much has gone on additional teachers and the reduction of the pupil/teacher ratio.

The Minister felt entitled to conclude: 'There has been a gradual improvement in standards.'

Of course, no such conclusion follows; unless, that is, we are intended to construe the word 'standards' as referring to nothing else but resource input. We are, without that proviso, simply not entitled to draw comfortable conclusions in this way; without, that is, any reference at all to evidence showing how many boys and girls have actually succeeded in learning what and how much.

At which point, if not long before, someone may object: 'But this is all perfectly obvious; we really did not need a philosopher to rabbit on about things of which every person of sense is already fully master.' To that the reply must be: either that obviousness in fact is, what so much else is nowadays falsely said to be, essentially relative; or else that, if the objector is right, the shortage of persons of sense must be even more severe than we had ever previously realized.

Suppose all this had always been obvious to everyone everywhere. Then how could we explain the facts: that so many people discuss public education in ways suggesting complete unfamiliarity with any of the points we have been making; and that we never encounter any attempts to demonstrate, however loosely, that these enormous increases in the public education budget have been rewarded with corresponding, or more than corresponding, increases in the amounts learnt.

Any such demonstration would have to be extremely rough and ready: both because of the impossibility of constructing standard units in which to sum the quantities of so many different kinds of learning output; and because, as was remarked earlier, present arrangements for monitoring this extremely diverse output are very incomplete, as well as very defective in other directions. The GCE 'A' level examination boards, for instance, acting on a remit from the whilom Secondary Schools Examinations Council, renewed when in 1964 the Schools Council took over, apparently award the same grades to the same percentages of all candidates in every successive year; thus invalidating straightforward, direct comparisons between the total numbers achieving particular grades in different years.[11]

Nevertheless, rough and ready though it would have to be, some such attempt to discover the actual direction and speed of movement is imperatively required of those pretending to be dedicated to the making of genuinely educational progress – as opposed, that is, to the maintenance and expansion both of the educational labour force and of the tax revenues by which it is funded.

(iii) By an easy and natural passage of ideas we come to the third example in this present Section IV. The National Union of Teachers (NUT) is by far the most numerous and powerful Edbiz pressure group. So let us take a short, distasteful look at the series of leaflets which the NUT Executive issued for their union's 1979 and 1980 'Campaign against the Cuts'.

Attention is here wholly concentrated upon resource input, with neither reference to nor question asked about the education output. In fury they tell the world that 'government policy means ... less education for your child'; and that 'Scrooge lived to regret his meanness.' They call for 'protest about the threat to education standards.' Yet the only standards over which they themselves appear in fact to be aroused, and to which what evidence they do produce actually is directed, are not educational at all: they are not, that is, standards achieved in and by teaching and learning. Instead it is all a matter of how many people are being or are to be employed as teachers; of how much money is to be spent on publicly provided school meals; and, generally, of the total public expenditure falling under the rubric 'Education'. The kindest although not by that token the fairest thing to be said about the entire campaign is that, while never actually attending to any questions about achieved educational output, they are always assuming, for no reason given or available, that educational goods are bound to be generated in exact and constant proportion to educational expenditures.

Really it is worse than this. For they tell us that 'there is no leeway in the service', and that 'after the years of cutback in education, there is no room for "economies" '. Yet never anywhere does the NUT make space for certain crucially relevant and in some cases directly falsifying facts: for instance, that over the last 30 years, public expenditure on education has *in real terms* multiplied fourfold; or that, in the same period, pupil/teacher ratios have fallen from 30.4 to 22.3 in primary schools – and from 21.1 to about 16.3 in secondary schools; or that spending on books and equipment could be roughly doubled at the price of returning to pupil/teacher ratios of only four or five years ago.[12] Were we to accept the criteria favoured by the NUT we should, on the basis of these too often forgotten facts, be able to say that educational standards have been rising at an unprecedented rate, have reached unprecedented heights, and are now – unless we have pretty substantial cuts to compensate for falling enrolments – set fair for a further recordbreaking rise.

V

Suppose, next, that we were to ask any high official in any of the relevant bureaucracies, either national or local, or almost any of their putative political masters, what are the aims of the entire public educational system, or of their own local element within that system. Then it is inconceivable that they could fail to include, somewhere near the top of their lists of objectives, something about achieving as near as may be universal minimum levels of literacy and numeracy; doubtless adding some pious yet nonetheless true truism about these being essentials for employability and effective citizenship in a modern industrial state.[13]

So, if the commitment to these modest objectives is as sincere and as absolute and as rational as all those responsible would wish us to believe, why are there no regular arrangements for discovering how many and what proportions of our young people are leaving school each year without attaining even such prescribed minimum levels? Only if and when satisfactory testing arrangements have been made will it become possible to construct reliable comparisons between successive cohorts; and, if it turns out that there is either no progress or insufficient progress, possible then to demand appropriate alterations in general schooling discipline and/or particular teaching methods.

(i) Again, as with the budgetary matters discussed in Section IV, the present situation is bound to astonish and appal anyone who is genuinely concerned for the education of all our children, and who approaches 'persuaded of these principles'. For the fact is that whenever public anxiety has risen enough to secure the appointment of a high level commission or committee, that improvised body has had to scratch around for evidence sufficient to warrant the forming of some sort of estimate of what the present position is, and of the directions in which things appear to be moving.

Now will it do to suggest that it is impossibly difficult to devise suitable tests; or inordinately expensive to give them to all, or to all whose performance in higher level examinations has not proved lower level testing to be superfluous. For competent and conscientious primary school teachers are devising and giving such tests all the time; while all that is needed for a reliable national scheme is standardisation and independent assessment, a large part of which could surely be computerised.

Lacking still any such comprehensive systems of actual testing, perhaps the best thing we have to go on is *Literacy and Numeracy: Evidence from the National Child Development Study* (London: Basic Skills Unit, 1983). In the present perspective the most remarkable features of this evidence are: that it is the evidence of a sample survey; and that the members of that sample were not actually given any tests. They were simply asked: whether they were themselves aware of any handicaps; and, if so, how severe and in what directions. There is nothing wrong with such investigations: sample surveys are a thrifty means of forming a rough estimate of distributions within the whole population; while, if you do want to know how people feel, it certainly is at least a good start to ask them to tell you. But none of this is any way to find out precisely who the actual adult illiterates and innumerates are, what schools they came from, and how the system might be so improved as to ensure that far fewer members of later cohorts are allowed to go out into the adult world so handicapped.

Equally remarkable is the fact that these facts were not underlined, nor was this moral taken, in the reports by the Education Correspondents, or in the leading articles of the general press. Those in *The Times* (22/VII/83) were on this occasion typical. Under the headline, 'At least 2*m*. illiterate adults in Britain, official report says', Lucy Hodges, the Education Correspondent, gave a very straight account: 'This estimate of the state of adult illiteracy ... confirms earlier figures which were based on guesswork'; and, 'Referring to a recent Gallup study on adult numeracy, which found young adults to be the most able group, the report says that in the adult population at large numeracy problems must be even more common.'

Neither in that report, nor in the leading article to which it concludes by referring, is there any suggestion that there should be standardised tests in the schools, tests which could constitute an actual census making all mere estimates obsolete. Yet this is what is done successfully, and without apparently any intolerable strain or difficulty, in Japan. There fantastically high levels of literacy are achieved in what is certainly one of the most if not the most difficult of all systems of writing.[14]

Again, anyone with a real concern that all our children should achieve at least a minimum standard of numeracy would surely have referred to the findings of the Institute of Mathematics.[15] They gave an actual test, 'designed so that virtually every pupil ought to be able to answer all the questions correctly', to a sample of children in schools maintained by five different LEAs. The results were generally abysmal, the worst coming from ILEA; which prides itself, as the NUT would wish us not to be reminded, on spending more per pupil than any other LEA.[16]

Another finding which – like all the rest – ought to have attracted much more attention than it did concerns pupil absenteeism. It is not surprising, although it should be disturbing, that this was much greater later in the school day, when the tests were given, than earlier, when the registers were called. Again it was ILEA where absenteeism was highest – a staggering 28%. I had this particular finding in mind in referring earlier to 'appropriate alterations' in both 'general schooling discipline and/or particular teaching methods'. For the most perfect teaching can scarcely be effective on those who cannot be induced to expose themselves to it!

(ii) Taking now a slightly different tack, we have to ask why we have no school-leaving examinations; examinations, that is, designed for and passable by that bottom 40% which cannot reasonably be expected to tackle either GCE or CSE. Certainly there is no lack of expressions of concern for this group. Indeed many of the militants of universal compulsory comprehensivisation appear to embrace no interest in anyone else. Yet if this really were not only a genuine but also an educational interest, then it could not but express itself in a desire to monitor the learning achievements and non-achievements of that presently submerged 40%.

So far only the present Minister, Sir Keith Joseph, has done or even said anything about providing such systematic monitoring – systematic monitoring through externally assessed examinations, that is, not mere pupil profiles unsupported by any independent verification. But, so far again, this initiative – like, it seems, his other initiatives – has not come to much. The only public indication of any consequent action has been a DES Press Notice (15 December 1982), announcing an experimental series of mathematical tests designed for members of this group. (Did the DES officials, I wonder, ask for help from the Institute of Mathematics; which, as we have seen, had designed and used and published just such a series several years earlier? Or did they, as in their preparation of a paper on education vouchers, refuse to go to any non-official sources?[17])

The problem of the bottom 40% came momentarily before the public mind once more with the publication of a report by S. J. Prais and K. Wagner, *Schooling Standards in Britain and Germany* (London: National Institute of Economic and Social Research, 1983). Commendably and, it must begin to seem, exceptionally these investigations did attend to what is actually being learnt rather than to how much is being spent. Their whole study is offered as 'Some Summary Comparisons Bearing on Economic Efficiency.' Naturally, such international comparisons are difficult. But, after all qualifications and allowances have been made, the general conclusions are as decisive as they are alarming: 'German pupils in the *lower half* of the ability range have a substantially higher level of attainment in basic arithmetical processes than *average* pupils in England'; and so on.

The media treatment of this NIESR report was, characteristically, misdirected. Some always uncritical attention was paid to the knee-jerk reactions of the NUT and its allies. They construed it as being –

like everything else – one more reason for further increasing the public education budget. The only commentator to see the report as pointing to a deficiency in our examination system was Anne Sofer.

In 'A German Lesson for Our Schools,' in *The Times* (1 November 1983), she wrote: 'The bottom half of the pupil population is failing so abysmally because they are subject to an examination system which is designed to pick out the brightest and fail the rest.' And she sees this as an expression of the attitudes of 'the conservative (with both a large and a small 'C') academic establishment', exclaiming 'Exams that everyone can pass. What nonsense!'

But it is, rather, Anne Sofer's commentary which is the true nonsense. For GCE 'O' level is NOT designed to be taken by all, but then inescapably failed by most. It is designed to be taken by ALL BUT ONLY those higher ability pupils who can reasonably be expected to pass. What is wrong with our system is: not that we make everyone take examinations which most – however hard they study and however well they are taught – are bound to plough; but that we fail to demand that everyone takes some examinations, but different examinations for different interests and different levels of ability.

To her credit, however, Anne Sofer does not argue, as has in fact frequently been argued even in official documents, that a decisive reason why we should develop a single, uniform system for examining at 16+ or whenever else is that abilities range over a continuum, across which the drawing of any sharp dividing line is more or less arbitrary. (Do such educational policy-makers actually need a philosopher to remind them that the dimensions of feet range similarly; but that this is an execrable reason for insisting that everyone be forced into boots or shoes of a single, uniform, standard size – all to be supplied, no doubt, by a subsidised state footwear monopoly?)[18]

What the Germans do have is a more varied and more comprehensive battery of examinations, not one single uniform examination with a minimum grade set so low that every candidate is bound to pass. As the NIESR report makes clear, candidates can and do fail all these different German examinations. Anne Sofer's protests notwithstanding, it would be – indeed, since nowadays it does sometimes happen, it is – a nonsense to conduct examinations which candidates cannot be any means contrive to fail. For how can a pass constitute an achievement, or serve as an indication of the attainment of any standard in anything, if such a 'pass' is awarded to all candidates quite irrespective of the work done or not done?

The true 'German lesson for our schools' is that we must at once so extend our not very systematic system of tests and examinations that it regularly and clearly reveals how much of what we want them to learn how many of our children are in fact learning. The mere extension of the system to include the bottom 40% would constitute a significant incentive both to them and to those whose job it is to teach them. While only the clearest, most comprehensive, and annually published evidence of success and failure can be expected to generate the political will to discover how to do better; and to make sure that we do in fact, and at last, nothing more nor less than actually do better.

VI

The third and last of the subjects for the application of 'these principles' which we shall consider here – albeit briefly – is the policy of universal compulsory comprehensivisation. This radical reorganisation has sometimes been described as a great experiment; just as in the 1920s and the 1930s Bolshevism was regularly characterised as 'that great social experiment in Russia'. But the approach of the chief enforcers has been no more inquiring and tentative in the former case than in the latter. There has in truth been precious little interest in monitoring the educational results, and absolutely no willingness even to consider any consequent halting or reversal of the implementation of this policy.

On the contrary: all calls for the publication of public examination results on any school by school basis used to be rejected; until, under a bitterly contested clause of the 1980 Act, this became mandatory. Note that in 1980 the NUT Executive called for 'total opposition' to this clause – for reasons about which we can with profit speculate. Since none of us have ever met Heads reluctant to boast of the successes of their schools, the presumption is that the supporters of concealment must have something to hide. Again: when, after Prime Minister Callaghan's Ruskin Speech (18 October 1976), the then Minister, Mrs Shirley Williams, set up the so-called Great Debate, this somehow found few, if any, participants eager to challenge a policy to which she and her then party were, and are, irrevocably committed.

If, and in so far as comprehensivisation is seen as a means to the educational end of ensuring that more of our children attain the highest learning levels of which they are capable; then the protagonists of this policy must be concerned to monitor its success or its failure, considered as a means to those most excellent and strictly educational ends. So when evidence turns up suggesting that the reorganisation is indeed having the desired effects; then they will, of course, be delighted. Their welcome will, nevertheless, not be uncritical. For, precisely to the extent that their commitment really is to the educational ends rather than to the policy itself, they cannot but be anxious lest this too welcome evidence may be inadequate, or may have been misinterpreted.

When evidence is produced suggesting that, on the contrary, the reorganisation is not having the desired effects; then they will be, most understandably, disappointed. How could they fail to be disappointed, on hearing the ungrateful news that something which they both expected and wanted to hapen is not, apparently, in fact happening? Naturally they will be eager to make an exhaustive critical examination of this evidence also.

What they certainly will not do – not, that is, if they really are dedicated to such generous and excellent educational ends – is to suppress or to howl down that disappointing evidence. Nor will they savage the people who have dared to try to bring it to their attention. For, precisely to the extent that their own commitment really is to the educational ends rather than to the policy itself; their concern actually to secure these ends will be far too strong to allow them to dismiss, unexamined, evidence which might show that pressing on with present policies must frustrate what truly are their own most cherished purposes. And, as for the people whose uncongenial evidence might reveal the misguidedness of present policies, how can any such ideal supporters of the reorganisation as we have been describing be anything but grateful to them?

Suppose now that, 'persuaded of these principles', we look at the actual recent reception of two relevant research reports. In the first case what was actually received, and accepted entirely uncritically at its own estimation of itself, was an article announcing the publication of a book by Jane Steedman (and others) *Progress in Secondary Schools* (London: National Children's Bureau, 1980). The comparatively short article summarising that massive, and notably expensive report appeared in the NCB's quarterly *Concern*, in the July 1980 issue. Long before anyone had had much chance to examine the primary document, it was being widely hailed in the press as having completely vindicated the whole comprehensive reorganisation: 'Report explodes comprehensive myth', the *Guardian* shouted; 'Clever children do as well in comprehensive as in grammar schools–study shows', said *The Times*; and so on. Only in the *Financial Times* were there clear indications that there had been some study of the data deployed, and the result was a carefully damning editorial.

Caroline Cox and John Marks, however, devoted the best part of their subsequent Long Vacations to *Progress in Secondary Schools*. The result was *Real Concern* (London: Centre for Policy Studies, 1980). This critique shows, to my mind quite decisively, that the conclusions of Steedman and her colleagues are not sustained even by their adjusted data, as presented in their report.

Real Concern got little attention in the specialist press, where most commentators continued to speak of the NCB work as authoritative, while dismissing any dissent as itself 'politically motivated'. Having made this charge such commentators should, surely, have revealed the individual political and interest group allegiances of *all* concerned, on *both* sides. Then, once these had been allowed to cancel out, they should have gone on to examine what everyone was, for whatever mixture of motives and interests, actually saying.

We are in fact given some clue to Steedman's own political commitments, and to their possible distorting effect, when she considers the fact that, on the NCB researchers' own showing, comprehensive parents are far more inclined to express dissatisfaction over the schooling of their children than the parents of children at either grammar or secondary modern schools: 'Of course it may be that indications of dissatisfaction reflect a certain criticality or involvement in decisions about schooling among parents which some schools would hope to foster' (p. 201).

The second of the recent reports is *Standards in English Schools*.[19] Both this and its authors have been subjected to an all-out campaign of vilification. At the stage when they felt moved to complain to the Press Council, the *Times Educational Supplement* had already printed 120 column inches of attack to a mere 20 of description and defence. Much was made – especially by spokespersons for the TUC Education Committee, for the Labour Party, and for the NUT – of a private document in which DES statisticians were said to have 'rubbished' this 'seriously flawed' and 'grossly incompetent' work.

Although the harried and hounded authors of *Standards in English Schools* were not to be permitted to see what was to them a professionally damaging, supposedly confidential departmental document, that document was widely leaked to Education Correspondents and other persons thought likely to be sympathetic. Fortunately one of the persons so privileged, jibbing at these dirty tricks, showed that critique to the authors criticised. They have since been able to demonstrate that what was asserted to be their fundamental fault was in fact a rather crude misunderstanding on the part of their DES critics.

These critics have since apologised, generously and publicly. They have withdrawn their original reservations, but not their several commendations of a path-breaking and exhaustive enterprise. These commendations had, of course, never been quoted by any of those making so much of the leaked critique. The DES statisticians have also agreed to release more information about the social class composition of school intakes, information which will make possible a more adequate allowance for differences in this respect. Despite all this, most if not all the various journals, spokespersons, and corres- pondents who seized so eagerly on a 'rubbishing' now admitted to have been itself seriously flawed, have been content to leave undone all the damage done by their onslaught on *Standards in English Schools*, and even continue to repeat the same charges.[20]

The final moral for us is that we cannot concede that those responding to the publication of those two research reports in the various sorts of uncurious and shabby ways just now described have been motivated by a strong and singleminded drive to secure that all our children reach the highest levels of learning achievement of which they are capable. Let it suffice for today to point out that some have adopted comprehensivisation, along with a more or less total rejec- tion of all selection, as an end seen as good in itself, rather than as a supposed means to further and more purely educational goods. To such persons, presumably, the news that some sorts of children, or even that all children, did worse under this preferred system would appear: not as a reason for abandoning a particular educational policy; but rather as a perhaps regretted cost of realising their own peculiar and by no means exclusively educational ideals.[21] Such would, I take it, be the stance adopted by John White, Reader in Philosophy of Education at the London Institute of Education. No doubt there are many who would echo his contention: 'Comprehen- sive schooling is an integral part of the socialist vision.'[22]

NOTES

1. It is in the comparative privacy of a footnote perhaps just worth emphasising, yet once more, that Hume was never so foolish as to maintain that every actual utterance in fact expresses a proposition which

is already and unambiguously of the one or the other kind. Here – as in his equally famous discussion of the relations or lack of relations between claims about what *is* and about what *ought* to be (*Treatise*, III(i)1) – Hume's point, surely, is: not that the distinction always is drawn, although it was left to him to notice both the fact and its significance; but rather that it always can and often should be so drawn? Especially, yet not only, in that second case some philosophers who think of themselves as highly sophisticated manage to misunderstand Hume; dismissing his contentions with a contempt which would indeed be well warranted if he had actually believed what they so superciliously mistake him to have been saying. See, for instance: J. R. Searle 'How to derive *ought* from *is*', comparing my 'On not deriving *ought* from *is*'; both in W. D. Hudson (ed.) *The Is/Ought Question* (London: Macmillan, 1969). Or see B. Gibbs *Freedom and Liberation* (Sussex University Press, 1976), pp. 115–1, comparing my '"Freedom is Slavery": a Slogan for Our New Philosopher Kings' in A. Phillips Griffiths (ed.) *Of Liberty* (Cambridge University Press, 1983) pp. 58–9.

2. See J. A. Schumpeter *Capitalism, Socialism and Democracy* (London: Allen & Unwin, 1963) esp. ch. VII.

3. Reprinted, in a revised version, in my *Sociology, Equality and Education* (London: Macmillan, 1976) ch. 6.

4. There is also some reason to believe that at least in some areas and with some people continuous as opposed to discontinuous feedback of information on success or failure tends, as a matter of contingent fact, to improve performance. Madsen Pirie, in *Trial and Error and the Idea of Progress* (La Salle, Illinois: Open Court, 1978) cites some experiments on efforts to acquire a simple skill, in which groups with discontinuous feedback 'improved over a dozen trials from being on target forty per cent of the time to achieving fifty per cent on target performance' while the groups with continuous feedback 'started with nearly fifty per cent success and improved it, over the same period, to sixty-four per cent success' (pp. 78–9 and 83).

5. *The Logic of Scientific Discovery* (London: Hutchinson, 1959) p. 278. That last statement would seem to imply that there neither is nor can be any such thing as scientific knowledge; nor, consequently, any growth thereof. I have tried to disembarrass Popper's account of this intolerable paradox, in my contribution to the *Proceedings of the Xth International Conference on the Unity of the Sciences: Seoul*, vol. II (New York: International Cultural Foundation, 1982) pp. 1263–81.

6. *The Open Society and its Enemies*, vol. I (London: Routledge & Kegan Paul, Fifth Edition, 1966) p. 160.

7. Ibid., p. 163.

8. C. A. R. Crosland *Socialism Now* (London: Cape, 1976), p. 20.

9. It is also, prior to all investigation, hugely implausible. For the great majority of British parents receive teaching services for their children free at the point of supply, and from monopolists who have only very recently – by the 1980 Education Act – begun to be compelled to reveal a modicum of information about their own effectiveness. For arguments in favour of the education voucher as a means of securing, among other

things, a more cost-effective public educational system, see my *Power to the People!* (London: Centre for Policy Studies, 1983). Also, for some information about very different results yielded by similar expenditures, see both one or two of the references given there and J. Marks, C. Cox, and M. Pomian-Srzednicki *Standards in English Schools* (London: National Council for Educational Standards, 1983).

10. Until very recently the weight of the (mainly North American) evidence seems to have been as much contrary to the second as to the first of Crosland's two assumptions; although this evidence has – surprise, surprise – been constantly ignored or rejected both by the teachers' unions and by the other supply side pressure groups.

    Thus the 1950 edition of the *Encyclopedia of Education Research*, after reviewing the work done in the previous fifty years, found: 'On the whole, the statistical findings definitely favor large classes at every level of instruction except the kindergarten. ... the general trend of evidence places the burden of proof squarely upon the proponents of small classes' (p. 212). When James S. Coleman, under the auspices of the US Office of Education, embarked upon the most extensive survey of American schools ever undertaken he certainly expected that it would demonstrate a strong resources/results relationship. Yet in the year following the publication of his report on *Equality of Education Opportunity* he confessed his amazement that 'the evidence revealed that within broad geographic regions, and for each racial and ethnic group, the physical and economic resources going into a school have very little relationship to the achievements coming out of it'. See his article 'Toward Open Schools' in *The Public Interest*, autumn 1967.

    Christopher Jencks, in summarising the ensuing national debate, concluded: 'Variations in schools' fiscal and human resources have very little effect on student achievement – probably even less than the Coleman report implied.' See his 'A Reappraisal of the Most Controversial Educational Document of Our Time' in the *New York Times Magazine* for 8 October 1969.

    But now compare, perhaps, G. V. Glass, L. S. Cahen, M. L. Smith and N. N. Filby *School Class Size: Research and Policy* (Beverly Hills, Ca.: Sage, 1982). It is also fair to add that in this country, and perhaps also in the USA, the possible effects of reductions in class size may have been masked or offset by declines in teacher quality consequent upon the drive to achieve that 'huge expansion in the supply'. Thus 'in 1975, over 40% of students accepted for teacher training courses did not even possess a GCE 'O' Level Certificate in Mathematics'. See Max Wilkinson *Lessons from Europe* (London: Centre for Policy Studies, 1977) p. 6 and *passim*.

11. After I had said this on an Open University TV programme – about education vouchers – the Senior Assistant Secretary of the Associated Examination Board wrote to me to protest that his board had never received any such remit. Instead it preferred to ask its examiners to attempt the immensely hard yet correspondingly worthwhile task of maintaining fixed standards from year to year. I am delighted to seize this first opportunity to give credit where credit is due.

12. See J. Marks and F. Naylor 'The National Union of Teachers – Professional Association or Trades Union or ... ?,' in C. Cox and J. Marks (Eds.) *The Right to Learn* (London: Centre for Policy Studies, 1981).

13. It is in the present context wryly amusing, if nothing else, that, in their eventually successful *Yes, Minister* campaign to render nugatory Sir Keith Joseph's original 'philosophical commitment' to the education voucher, DES officials objected that a voucher system could not be guaranteed to meet 'the needs of employers'. See Paragraph 12 of the 'DES Document' reprinted at pp. 35–7 of *NCES Bulletin No 6*, December 1982. There is what I like to think a totally devastating critique of this 'DES Document' at pp. 3–7 of that same issue. Arthur Seldon is currently preparing for the Institute of Economic Affairs a study of this DES campaign.

14. I write with feeling and authority since most of my own service in World War II was work on written Japanese!

15. This report is most easily found reprinted as chapter IV of C. Cox and J. Marks (eds.) *The Right to Learn* (London: Centre for Policy Studies, 1982).

16. *The Times* for the previous day (21/VII/83), under the headline 'Cuts are endangering standards in schools, inspectors say', printed an account of the report of Her Majesty's Inspectors on the *Effects of Local Expenditure Policies on the Education Service in England in 1982* (Stanmore: DES, 1983). In this account Lucy Hodges, perhaps faithfully following an official lead, simply identifies standards in schools: not with quality of learning achievement; but with quantity of resource input. Certainly in the previous year the Inspectorate had reproached four unnamed LEAs for no other or educationally more relevant reason than that they were spending less per pupil. Nevertheless one might have hoped, although one could scarcely have expected, that an Education Correspondent would have noticed, and maybe reproached, this concentration on the input as opposed to the output.

17. See note 13, above.

18. Anyone who truly is in need of such philosophical assistance may find it in, for instance, my *Thinking about Thinking* (London: Collins Fontana, 1975) SS 7.13–7.24.

19. See note 9, above.

20. The fullest generally available treatments of this affair at the time of writing were two: first, an article in *The Times* (8 August 1983) by Ronald Butt and not – significantly – by their Education Correspondent; and, second, an imaginative reconstruction in *The Sunday Times* (2 December 1983) by the authors of *Yes, Minister* and not – still more significantly – by their Education Correspondent.

Cox and Marks will be publishing in the *Oxford Review of Education*, a survey of all the research evidence on the educational effects of comprehensive reorganisation. They are also preparing a study of the whole campaign to discredit *Standards in English Schools*.

21. It would, nevertheless, be a grievous mistake to think that such comparative indifference on their part to what others will regard as

lamentable educational consequences will necessarily make them complacent towards the publicising of any findings suggesting that there are
indeed consequences of this kind. On the contrary: the comprehensive
lobby has the best of reasons to fear the reactions to such findings of that
great majority of our people to whom comprehensivisation and the
destruction of the maintained selective schools was sold, if indeed it ever
has been sold, not as a good in itself but as a supposed means to
improved educational achievement. (See, on the operations of this lobby
and on related matters, Beverley Shaw *Comprehensive Schooling: the
Impossible Dream?* (Oxford: Blackwell, 1983).

22. In 'Tyndale and the Left,' in *Forum*, vol. 19, p. 60. I owe this reference
to Beverley Shaw, op. cit, pp. 23–4 and 78.

3 Education as a Positional Good

MARTIN HOLLIS

It is sports' day at Llanabba Castle preparatory school. The Three Miles Open race has just been run, with young Clutterbuck first home. But the day's even tenor is jarred, when Lady Circumference accuses him of skipping a lap. Tempers rise and Dr Fagan, the headmaster, hastens to join the group round the winning post.

> 'If there is a disputed decision,' he said genially, 'they shall race again.'
> 'Percy has won already,' said Mr. Clutterbuck. 'He has been adjudged the winner.'
> 'Spendid! Splendid! A promising little athlete. I congratulate you, Clutterbuck'.
> 'But he ran only five laps,' said Lady Circumference.
> 'Then clearly he has won the five furlongs, a very exacting length.'
> 'But the other boys,' said Lady Circumference, almost beside herself with rage, 'have run six lengths.'
> 'Then they,' said the Doctor imperturbably, 'are first, second, third, fourth and fifth respectively in the Three Miles. Clearly there has been some confusion. Diana, I think we might now serve tea.'[1]

Clutterbuck is not only a promising little athlete. He is also a promising little student of society. He has spotted that the race need not be to the swift nor the battle to the strong. If a trophy is to be the reward of the virtuous, then there may be more efficient ways of gaining that reward. Clutterbuck has exploited a weakness in the whole idea of cashable symbols of inner moral fibre. Imperturbably the headmaster restores the facade and, being unable to amend the reality, offers tea. Outraged sportsmanship still glitters in every eye but the positional element in education has been duly draped with cucumber sandwiches. It is our grave task to disinter it.[2]

Education has social functions which go unmentioned on speech day, when we praise the virtues of sportsmanship as preparation for the game of life. There is a tension between the moral aims of the educator and the conditions on which the larger society will hire his services. That is no revelation. But I shall start by rehearsing the thought, as a neat way of introducing the idea of a positional element in education. Once introduced, the idea will be abstracted and then put to less familiar use. Education prepares children for a place amid a division of labour and the goods, which it offers under this head, are uncontentiously positional, at least in part. It also tries to nurture the soul, however, and the goods of that realm are supposed to be intrinsic. This piety will, I hope, turn out more comforting than true. To lay the groundwork, let us start with the familiar positional element.

A 'positional good', defined loosely for the moment, is a good, valuable to some people only on condition that others do not have it.[3] Prizes are a ready example, since winners need losers. (Clutterbuck's prize was no doubt worthless, since he was the only contender in the five furlong race. But Lady Circumference was right to expostulate, since outsiders might not know it.) Most jobs require some basic level of skill but, beyond that, they are awarded after competition to the applicant best equipped in comparison with his fellows. Schools have the obvious task of equipping applicants. They also have the less obvious task of reducing their number. So the good conferred by education is both overtly positional and, in subtler ways, latently positional too. An example will save a ton of abstractions.

A city council wants a junior manager in its housing department, advertises and has a flood of applications. All are from youngish, greenish, keenish persons, not readily distinguishable. In search of the fittest, the selectors look to the educational record, thus manifestly seeking the brightest and latently cutting down the field to manageable size. But now there is a decision of policy to make. The brighter applicants fall into two broad groups. Some have left school at sixteen, passably literate and numerate, and have since been rent collectors or clerks, thus serving a relevant apprenticeship. Others are graduates with degrees in, say, social science and know less of the ropes but more of the system. Which group is the fitter? In theory there is no definite answer, since formal schooling is not always an advance on the school of life. In practice, however, graduates will probably be preferred, since housing management is fast becoming a graduate profession, like so many others. Further education will then have been an advantage.

The advantage is not baseless. In so far as a degree certifies useful knowledge and reflective skill, and provided the ropes can be learnt on the job, the higher the qualification the better. So there is a clear sense in which the absolute level of performance can be raised by education. But neither is the advantage wholly justified on absolute grounds. Education, notoriously, also acts as a filter, whose merits may have little to do with knowledge and skill. When Gideon had to pick 300 men for an attack on the Midianites and had 700 qualified applicants, the Lord commanded him to let all drink at the river and to choose those who lapped water like dogs (of whom there turned out to be just 300 – *Judges* 7:1–7). Housing managers cannot be winnowed in this way without scandal, and certificates have the merit of being a legitimating filter. Also it suits those already *en poste* at the city hall for the profession to become graduate. It strengthens the case for higher salaries all round and tightens the grip on future access. Here education is conferring relative advantage and the connection between relative and absolute need be no more than a token one of legitimacy. Otherwise *Decline and Fall* would not be funny and it is notable that it still has an edge, even though, fifty years after its publication, Dr Fagan and Llanabba Castle are hardly more typical of English life than Lord Emsworth and Blandings.

This latently positional function of education in supplying a filter is of general service to the division of labour. Employers pay taxes partly so that there are schools to pre-select labour for them. Schools earn their bread and butter therefore by differentiating and ranking their students. Students demand of schools to be equipped for success in the division of labour. This symbiosis is somewhat discreet and, when talked about, is usually dressed in an absolutist language of quality, specialisation and opportunity. But it is undeniably at work. Nor is it a discreditable price for teachers to pay for their bread and butter, since it also lets them shape society a generation hence and in ways less constrained by the present job market. Yet it does have wry effects. For instance the better the comprehensive schools do in raising the number of well qualified applicants for the nation's jobs, the less their efforts will count when it comes to placing them. For, faced with surplus applicants, selectors look for qualities which favour some only because others lack them. The combination of silicon chips with improved comprehensive schooling is bound to make a headmaster's uplifting speeches much harder to write.

This, in rapid caricature, is the familiar sense in which education confers positional goods on those who go on to apply for jobs. Its benefits cannot accrue to everyone. Not all its benefits are positional but some certainly are. At any rate I shall not doubt it here; and the rest of the chapter is concerned not with whether there is any positional aspect to education but with how deep it goes. To set about an answer, we next need a more exact notion of a positional good.

Fred Hirsch puts the idea in a nutshell by remarking, 'if everyone stands on tiptoe, no one sees better' (*Social Limits to Growth*, p. 5). Standing on tiptoe is a good for some but only if others stay put. So positional goods are scarce goods. Not all goods are scarce; nor are all scarce goods positional. For instance oxygen in the air is a good without being scarce; busts of Wittgenstein are scarce without being positional. Numbered lithographs, on the other hand, are positional, since the more there are, the less each is valued. The numbering raises the value by guaranteeing a limited stock and, while everyone could own a mere print, not everyone could enjoy a guarantee that not everyone owns one. Hirsch calls this element 'social scarcity' and it accompanies most of the goods which we all ask of economic growth, he says. Consequently any hope that growth will satisfy all wants is doomed to be dashed.

He distinguishes between a 'direct' and an 'incidental' form of social scarcity. It is direct when satisfaction derives from the scarcity itself, as with the snob factor in the numbering of lithographs. Value here derives typically, he says, from motives like 'envy, emulation and pride'. Scarcity is incidental when value stems from an inherent characteristic of the good but is influenced by crowding. Incidental scarcity subdivides into 'physical congestion', as when the fun of motoring declines as the traffic thickens, and 'social congestion', as when the pleasure of conducting an orchestra has to be shared with a fellow conductor. The goals of economic growth are attended, in his view, by direct and incidental scarcity, both physical and social.

That covers the implications of treating education as a filter. In so far as certificates are prizes, their value is directly positional. In so far as they certify a level of skill, whose pleasure in acquisition and practice is lessened but not destroyed by crowding, their value is incidentally positional. But the distinction is not as sharp as I shall need. So let us be more formal. Anything is a good for a person, if he would rather have it than be without it. (What, if anything, he is willing to pay for it is another matter.) That can be expressed as a simple preference ordering of two states, his having it above his not having it. For a positional good three (or more) states are involved:

(1) his having it and others not,
(2) everyone having it,
(3) no one having it.

(Here (1) must outrank (2) and (3); but (2) and (3) can be in any order.) The distinction between direct and incidental scarcity can now be neatly put as one between necessary and contingent. Prizes necessarily cease to be goods, if everyone has them. Indeed they cease to be prizes. Motoring contingently stops being a pleasure, if everyone motors, because there happen not to be enough roads. So more roads would restore the fun, whereas more prizes would dilute the glory.

I have just made it the mark of a good that someone wants it. That is the economist's usage, with no implication that goods must be valuable as well as valued. So, even if education is a positional good in the economic sense, it will not follow that the 'true' goods to be had from education are positional. Nonetheless I shall contend that they are. The familiar case, just rehearsed, concerns the educator's task in supplying the job market. I turn now to his other task, the nurture of the soul. Here too, I maintain, there is a positional moral economy. (The 'too' is deliberate – where work is a mere instrument, something is lacking from the moral life.) To make the case, I shall consider the nurture of the soul under three aspects. The first is 'talent', referring to the peculiar abilities, practical, cognitive and aesthetic, of each child, which give each its own way of self-expression and self-development. The second is 'culture', meaning an awareness of the habits and traditions of peoples and especially of our own society. The third is 'virtue' or the fostering of moral beliefs and sentiments, so that the educated adult shall not use his talents and cultural knowledge merely to exploit other people better. I shall not maintain that all the goods of the soul are positional; but it is the heartiest platitude of the speech-day oration that none of them is and I shall try to disprove this soothing view in all three departments.

'Talent' offers the easiest target, owing to a relativity about its supply. A talent is a skill but not every skill is a talent. Little Johnny took some years to master the skill of walking upright but he did not thereby develop a talent for it. Too many other children can walk upright too and he is nothing out of the ordinary or peculiar. Had he been born crippled, then the skill is harder to acquire and success comes closer to being a talent. But that is because the reference group is now severely handicapped children, among whom he might indeed be out of the ordinary. The possessor of a talent has to be in a minority of some population (usually of the population at large). In classing a skill as a talent, then, we imply that not everyone has it. To this extent talents are directly positional.

I do not suggest that a skill has to be valued, marketable or morally worthy before it can be a talent. There is no market for hand-engraving the Lord's prayer on the head of a pin. The shrinking of human heads gains no moral credit. Yet both activities are, I presume, talents, since those who can perform them have skill in an unusual degree. So it may seem wholly innocuous to point the positional element out. In so far as talents are useful to the soul in the pursuit of self-development, it looks as if a skill is, in any case, as useful as a talent. The question seems solely whether there is satisfaction in engraving the Lord's prayer or shrinking heads; and, if there is, each soul could be as well nurtured, if all others did it too.

That is to take too etherial a view, however. Most talents need resources and most resources are scarce (whether contingently, like costly engraving tools, or necessarily, like human heads for use by human headshrinkers). In heaven, perhaps, everyone can learn the harp and play it eternally amid universal rejoicing. But on earth harps are expensive and, even were they not, they take much time to learn and practice. Johnny's skill has an opportunity cost, depending partly on what he would otherwise do with the time and money, partly on how many other promising little harpists there are. So one way of nurturing this soul, which could be universal in heaven, is positional on earth. Whether he has a talent and whether it is worth cultivating are both comparative questions.

There is also a limit to the fun to be had from playing a lone harp to oneself. Even in heaven there are massed harps and even there a few trumpets are used for contrast. Also the lack of an audience must be rather trying. On earth talents plainly need coordination. The harpist needs an orchestra, conductor and listeners. Every talented goal-keeper needs the services of twenty-one other players and a referee. Every Romeo needs his Juliet, every burglar his fence. Talents usually require complementary talents and some orchestration. Their value is absolute neither to others nor to the possessor himself. Admittedly the element of complementarity is not yet a positional one. The question is not 'What if everyone played the harp?' but 'What if no one played anything else?' But, since talents need an investment of time, effort and cash, we can take it that, if everyone did master the harp, no one would manage the rest. So the distributional requirements of complementarity do make the talent positional. A talent which is frustrated is a familiar educator's problem and one not always to be solved by removing the frustration. There is no point in nurturing the soul in talents which bring no satisfaction and satisfaction can depend on the state of the market.

The positional element in talents thus has, so to speak, a vertical and a horizontal dimension. Vertically, Johnny must excel others. This is partly a matter of logic – only in a very rare school can he twentieth best goalkeeper be said to have a talent – and partly a practical point – the twentieth goalkeeper gets little chance to play. Horizontally, the complementary jobs must be done – there must be those twenty-one other players and a referee – before the talent is worth having. So a talent will typically need backing with manpower and resources and its value in the self-development of Johnny is conditional on what talents are nurtured in others. The soul in this aspect develops through both competition and cooperation. The moral to be drawn is not that ideally an all-powerful state should decree the exact number of harpists or goalkeepers required. That would be too stifling to contemplate. But the filtering will be done somehow – it is not luck which sees to it that each football team has just one goalkeeper. Those who nurture talents in children need a shrewd idea of the system of filters and the state of the talent market. Neither in logic nor in practice should they think of themselves as doing what is intrinsically best for an isolated soul. Bachelors with a detailed blueprint for their uniquely possible soul mate are likely to stay bachelors and serve them right; but those with an easier sense that many marriages can be made on earth fare better. So too the wise child is willing to cultivate whatever talents the positional economy will support. For, I submit, self-development has an unmistakable element of the positional in it.

The second heading is 'Culture' or the understanding to be instilled in children of themselves, their neighbours, their society and mankind at large. To flourish as persons they must know their roots, the reasons historical and contemporary why their social world is as it is. I shall not be precise about the ingredients. Roughly, cultural understanding is in part down to earth and in part to do with aspirations. There is practical knowledge to be gained, for instance of trades unions, industry, government, elections and the law. These matters have a history, which still enables and constrains all who seek work, home and amusement in our society. Also Britain is a polyglot island from some points of view and, from others, not an island at all but an outpost of a larger European or world community. Some grasp, social and historical, of such components of social life is directly useful. At the same time culture includes what people have aspired to and it is a practical fact that man does not live by bread alone. Religion, ethical belief, art and poetry, the pursuit of meaning in life are very much a part of what makes people tick and hence of what children need to know about. Nor are these aspirations simply speech-day solemnities or the hollow incantations of Sunday sermons. Everyone attaches meaning to something in life and does so in an everyday sort of way, which makes the contacts of daily life into cultural contacts too. Thus culture is an important part of the world which children inherit and one which conditions their own hopes too. But, since time is short, I shall not be more specific, trusting that is enough has been said to mark the aspect of the nurture of the soul, which I have in mind.

Let us take it as read that cultural understanding is a good. How far is it a positional one? In some degree, I admit at once, it is not positional at all. Everyone needs a measure of this sort of understanding to function in society with even modest autonomy. No-one can make a go of personal life in a cultural vacuum. Even an indrawn family lives in a changing world and even on one's own patch an awareness of how others see things is essential. But these obvious truths take us only so far and, for the rest, there is, I believe, a positional element in the sort of knowledge to which 'culture' gestures. At some risk of overplaying my hand, therefore, I shall stress the positional character of this good.

Cultural understanding involves both knowing that and knowing how. The question is whether it also involves knowing better than others. To lead into it, let us start with positional knowledge in general. The prime example is knowing a secret, since a secret known to all is a secret no longer. Economically speaking, knowledge often functions as a commodity. It is costly to acquire, commands a share of the return on the product of commerce and, more simply, can be bought and sold on its own. Well-designed mailing lists, for example, are bought and sold, and all sorts of agencies make a living only because they know something which other people do not. Indeed, if we turn to pure economic theory, the whole idea of perfect information is really very odd, even as a limiting or ideal condition in the most simplified and abstract model. For it is at least arguable that no market would function at all, if everyone knew whatever anyone else knew. So there is nothing outré about the idea of knowledge which is commercially worth having only because it is scarce. In our usual thoughts about science, on the other hand, secrets are, or should be, nature's alone. There is no virtue in keeping one's discoveries to oneself; or rather, in so far as there is, it is for commercial or political rather than for scientific reasons. In an ideal scientific world every discovery would be made public at once and that would be of benefit to everyone.

Given this contrast, most of us will no doubt want to construe cultural understanding by analogy with science rather than commerce. Nor shall I dissent in the end. But it is worth noting that it can function commercially. The British class and status system is not fully meritocratic. Aitches can be dropped pretty freely nowadays but it remains important to have the proper background and attitudes for one's circle. Dr Fagan made his living from the fact and Llanabba Castle would have gone bankrupt at once without it. Although that is now just a comic allusion, there are still schools which make part of their living from the sale of exclusive and excluding culture. Cultural advantage can still be part of what fee-paying parents get for their money. Even within the state system one motive for comprehensive education has been an objection to the use of cultural differences by too many grammar school teachers as a way of making their pupils behave better than the mob in the secondary modern down the road. I claim no great weight for these points. But they remain more than trifling, while culture still functions as a constraint on meritocracy. While the filtering into jobs, which meritocracy would do on IQ + ability, is partly done by tests of cultural understanding, there is bound to be some positional element in this sort of knowledge.

In echo of what was said about talents, cultural advantage is the 'vertical' dimension. There is also a 'horizontal' dimension. What knowledge is worth acquiring depends on who else knows what. It is not good for the soul to learn Icelandic, unless one proposes to mix with Icelanders or read their literature. At the very least there must be other persons with the same enthusiasm, so that, if real Icelanders are desperately scarce, an Icelandic Society can keep a candle in the window. Otherwise whatever universal value there is in Icelandic studies will be better had from some other activity which has the same inherent interest and more chances of contact. In other words, to say that some cultural understanding is crucial for all is not to claim that the same diet should be given to everyone. A variety of diets is essential and that raises questions of coordination. Coordination could be left to luck but there is no reason to expect much of luck as a solution. As with talents earlier, I am not going on to argue that the problem should therefore be handed over to an autocratic ministry of culture. The point is solely that the value of culture to each is a function of the overall pattern. Once that is granted, a positional element can be seen.

Like other educational activities, culture has costs in provision. Think of university funding. Crudely, the government will pay for only so much understanding, even if broadly in favour of it. Up to a point the supply of places and tutors responds to demand. A craze for Mithraism calls forth lecturers in Mithraic studies. But it does so only up to a point. Then the government cries 'halt!' and would-be Mithraists are in competition. Sixth-form teachers take note before letting Johnny embark on a Mithraic 'A' level, just as they require several interested pupils before putting Mithras on the curriculum at all. Resources are given to universities according to some notion of overall pattern of the cultural understanding worth paying for. From the paymaster's angle, the relativities in each decision are plain; and they are no less real because a kind of haphazard pluralism is practised. The overall pattern affects the value of each subject as a way to cultural understanding, just as some kinds of flowers will get pollinated only in the right sort of mixed border.

The paymasters are not being unreasonable. Resources are limited. An extra Mithraist replaces an extra plumber somehow, somewhere, by a series of ricochets at the margins of budets. Every allocation has an opportunity cost. A moral and political decision has been made about priorities. This is visibly so in countries where the state explicitly chooses the cultural pattern. In countries which leave such things to markets or osmosis or hazard, it is still so, since the choice of that method is still a moral and political choice[4]. Hence, whatever the inherent value of cultural understanding to the soul, its actual value varies with political decisions which shape the cultural pattern. So a decision about social priorities affects different pieces of cultural knowledge differently and that too is best expressed by saying that part of the value of understanding ancient Rome or trades unions or Rastafarianism is positional. Here again the souls being nurtured are not those of hermits.

Even with the main dimension horizontal, and the positional element one of knowing different rather than knowing better, the moral is striking. It is that benefit to each depends on benefit to all, whereas benefit to all does not guarantee benefit to each. This old and annoying paradox of political ethics is more familiar under headings like freedom, welfare and justice. (For instance it benefits all if (and only if) all adhere to an incomes policy; but it benefits some more, if others adhere to it while they do not. No one has yet devised a system of rules to serve the general welfare which leaves no room for protest on behalf of individual freedom.) Here it is again in less familiar guise and educators must wrestle with it. That is yet another consequence of the fact that no man is an island.

Thirdly there is virtue. Every teacher tries to instil or elicit it, hoping to see his pupils make moral progress towards becoming good men and women. He wants it for all of them and believes deeply that it is within reach of all. So a positional element in virtue would be disconcerting. Yet it does seem to me to be there.

To stake out the ground, let us start with the minor virtue of courtesy. On the whole there is, I take it, no reason why everyone should not treat everyone courteously and, when they do, the small wheels of social life turn easily. But the process does have an occasional quirk. For example it is good manners to let others through a doorway first; but, if everyone insisted on it, doorways would become a major hazard to the good life. This 'after-you-Cecil' – 'No after-you-Claud' aspect of things is quite common in virtues connected with altruism and self-effacement. If everyone puts the interests of others before his own, no one's interests are served. If everyone values himself below others, the currency of respect collapses. Anyone who has tried to organise an outing for a group of determinedly unselfish people will know how maddening it can be. Such examples are no doubt trivial but they show how a virtue might cease to be a virtue, if everyone practised it.

That suggests at least a horizontal dimension. The value of a talent to each person depended on a spread of a variety of talents and the value of a cultural investment depended on a similar variety. So too there are complementary virtues. Typically they are those of roles. The film director should be imaginative and the producer painstaking; the firm's manager ruthless and its personnel officer sympathetic; and so forth. A gap in the set of virtues diminishes the others. This may seem to arise because roles often interrelate for a specific purpose, like making a film or running a corporation. But it will generalise, at any rate to much broader purposes like organising a successful community. From Plato onwards thinkers have held that the Good Society must flourish in several departments, each requiring particular virtues in its citizens. Those virtues need not or even cannot be displayed by each citizen. In the *Republic*, for example, guardians are wise, soldiers brave, and the working population acquisitive. Each class specialises for the sake of a common good, which will be served only if no class fails. Plato is not everyone's ideal moralist but he is not alone in thinking that virtues need not be identical for everyone. In any such reckoning the worth of each will depend on the existence of others.

A vertical dimension is harder to find. The pure case would be where the exhortation to virtue is like a command with a comparative in it. For instance, if 'Be frugal!' meant 'eat less than the average person', it would become annihilating when taken seriously by all. But I cannot plausibly argue in general that 'Be good!' means 'Be better than the next man!' nor can I hit upon any specific virtue with a comparative directly built into it. 'Keep up with the Joneses!' is not the form of the categorical imperative. Nonetheless there are virtues which cannot be practised by all for indirect reasons. It has often been noticed that some private virtues sum to public vices. Thrift, for example, is commended by the Protestant ethic, although universal thrift would destroy the economy and, with it, the value of thrift to each saver. Charity too has been held to become bad for the receiver in excess and a corresponding limit set to the activities of a Welfare State. What is a virtue in each person can thus cease to be one, when all practise it. Similarly there are virtues which can be exercised by individuals only in moderation. Firmness becomes obstinacy after a point, impartiality turns to callousness, independence of spirit passes into pride. Individual moderation does not set a problem, since each pupil can learn to monitor his own performance, but collective moderation does, since it threatens to replace moral worth with moral luck for individual actions.

The threat being posed is to the idea of virtue as obedience to a universal moral law, whatever the consequences. In bidding someone be thrifty, we cannot be telling him to act as if in a world where everyone was thrifty. In such a world thrift would not be a virtue. Even more instructive, however, is the thought that much of what would be virtuous, if everyone did it, can cease to be virtuous, when not universally practised. For instance let us agree that honesty is a virtue, if all are honest. Yet it does not follow that the more people are honest (in both senses of the clause) the better it is. In an imperfect world there is often merit in being dishonest. When the

Gestapo pose as friends of a hidden Jew and ask his whereabouts, they should, I take it, be given a dishonest answer. The value of honesty varies with consequences and in practicular with the honesty of the other party. Perhaps we should sometimes, or even often, return good for evil. But I defy anyone to prove that we should always do so and, short of that, it becomes an important part of a moral education to know when (to put it paradoxically) it is virtuous to be wicked.

This case is complicated because I defined a positional virtue as one which would cease to be a virtue if everyone practised it. Honesty does not have this feature but dishonesty has the corresponding one that in a sufficiently imperfect world it ceases to be a vice. The general point is that moral rules often need to take account of the level of compliance with them. This echoes a familiar criticism of rule utilitarianism, that acting on rules which would produce the greatest good, if all obeyed them, may be a mistake, if others do not. To that I add the enjoyable thought that virtue in a world of imperfect compliance can be vice in a perfect world. Necessarily positional virtues are, I admit, hard to find. (If everyone jumps in to save a child from drowning, the poor mite will be drowned in the rush; but I cannot plausibly build on that.) But contingently positional ones are common, since we happen to live in a world where a pig-headed determination to do good has markedly inferior effects.

Moral education, then, does not consist in equipping children with the moral consistency of a rhinoceros. What is to be classed as a virtue, how high a particular virtue is to be ranked and when precisely it is to be translated into action are all matters depending on the state of the outside world. We hope that our children will leave the world a better place than they found it. So by all means let us fill them with unswerving moral concern. But let us not suppose that they must therefore refuse to be devious. To practice positional virtues in an imperfect world they will need the guile of serpents.

On these grounds, then, I think that all three aspects of the nurture of the soul have positional elements. Each aspect yields particular reasons but there are also two general ones, which are worth stressing by way of summary. One is that the soul needs a provision of resources, limited in supply and with rival uses. The other is that souls need orchestrating, in that the proper nurture of each depends on what is done about others. Let us ask what all this implies for the theory of education.

It certainly implies a more social and political view of the educated person than is usual in speaking of the moral education of the soul. The value of what is learnt becomes conditional in unexpected ways. Such interdependence has always been plain enough for the practical, division-of-labour job of education in a society needing not too many and not too few workers, each after their trade or profession. The shape of the job market is decided outside schools or left to the workings of an external economy and teachers see it as their task to respond. Having served Mammon by teaching economics and wood-work, however, the teacher now turns to higher things. For the nurture of souls, a language of individual differences, spiritual values and intrinsic goods is spoken. But, if my argument stands, this contrast is spurious. Souls too need to be equipped for an outside world, marked by a moral division of labour, and, in equipping them, teachers are shaping citizens who will express themselves in their work. There is a difference in power, since the job market is immediate and largely externally given, whereas today's children embody tomorrow's values and the teacher has a freer hand. But the broad character of the enterprise is the same and the social and political tests of whether the teacher has done his duty are merely less obvious.

It may sound as if I am calling for centralised state control of the nurture of the soul. I am not. Just as in economics total planning is not the only alternative to *laissez-faire*, so too the orchestration of souls has other solutions (I hope). But I do want to press the analogy between the two realms. In their dealings with Mammon, educators usually accept that people need skills which the economy will pay to employ and will be happier if their wants are broadly those which the economy can satisfy. Since neither skills nor wants are innate, at least not in any precise form, schools have some choice about which to emphasise and, on the whole, are content to let an outside voice call the tune. They could try refusing. They could teach skills of use only to a different sort of economy and could instil wants which only an alternative society would satisfy. There would be dreadful com-plaints, not least from the pupils, but they could. In practice, however, they accept that their job is an unsubversive, although not slavish, one of support for the present system. The demands of economy and government are treated as legitimate constraints on education.

For the nurture of the soul the theoretical position is edgier. In practice teachers are usually unsubversive here too, since they share enough of the values of the larger society to be willing to school their pupils in them. But, in theory, this side of an education is not supposed to be instrumental in the same way. The teacher has an almost priestly duty to arm his charges against corrupt values and to resist political pressures. At any rate this is a common view of his task. Yet he does also recognise some outside demands as legitimate and is willing, for instance, to instil a greater respect for Christian or Islamic doctrines than he may feel himself. The notional compromise is that he shall teach about various ethical, religious and political points of view without committing himself. But this distinction of first- from second-order instruction is widely felt to be more convenient than coherent.

Aided by discussion of positional goods, we can see one major reason for the edginess. The positional elements in talent, culture and virtue mean that the teacher's success is not within his control. It depends on the state of competition and coordination, both of which depend greatly on the shape of the larger society. This makes it unclear why it is not his duty here, too, merely to respond to the larger society by producing souls which will fit cosily into it. In a consumer society should he not mould his pupils to care deeply about fishfingers and furniture polish too? In terms of the orchestral analogy, it would seemingly be a failure on his part to produce musicians who play instruments for which there is no demand or play them better than the orchestra needs. The positional character of educational goods implies that each pupil will flourish in proportion as he then fits into the social system but seems not to imply any measure of a social system beyond how smoothly it functions.

I wish I could be surer how to reply. The premise is that the flourishing (or *eudaimonia*) of the soul is a matter of a person's relations with others within a particular social scheme of values and practices. I accept the premise. The apparent conclusion is that any set of relations which works is as good as any other and that the task of a moral education is to supply the bits. I reject the conclusion. Why, then, does it not follow? Perhaps the answer is that *eudaimonia* cannot be secured by frontal assault. Both collectively and personally it is essentially a byproduct of decisions taken with the good life no more than partly in mind. It is often remarked that those who aim at happiness are bound to miss it, whereas those with other and more selfless aims will find themselves happy in their pursuit. If that is true, there may be a similar case for concluding that essentially social beings, whose spiritual success depends on orchestration, are nonetheless best served by an open and liberal society. At any rate there are still the classic arguments of Mill's *On Liberty* to appeal to in urging that tolerance, experiment and spontaneity are useful in every kind of political and social order. They are not foiled just because the goods of education are often positional nor because the nurture of the soul is of legitimate political concern.

We began with the virtue of sportsmanship and young Clutterbuck's insight into it. Sportsmanship is meant both to make us play better and to give us peace of mind when we lose. Clutterbuck found it intrinsically useful on neither count and extrinsically clearly inferior to cheating as a way of winning prizes. If his prize was not worth having that shows either how mistaken he was or that he should have fixed the race more thoroughly. But which? The speech-day answer springs, of course, to every lip. Yet he was awkwardly right about the positional character of much in education. Moreover, what set off as a cynic's argument about outward symbols has ended as one about inner graces. So it looks as if he may have been too right for our comfort in a world where there are legitimate external tests of talent, culture and virtue. I wonder what became of him. I rather fear that he grew up to be Secretary of State for Education.

NOTES

1. Evelyn Waugh, *Decline and Fall*, (Harmondsworth: Penguin, 1951) ch. 8.
2. I would like to thank Robert Dearden and others, whose comments on the draft read to the Philosophy of Education Society of Great Britain have been very helpful.
3. I am following gratefully Fred Hirsh, *Social Limits to Growth* (London, Routledge & Kegan Paul, 1977).
4. My reasons for saying this are to the found in 'The Pen and the Purse', *Proceedings of the Philosophy of Education Society of Great Britain*, vol. v, no. 2, (1971). See also John Wilson's reply in vol. ix, no. 1. (1975) and my answer in vol. x (1976).

Part II
Rationality, Understanding and Education

4 The Transmission of Knowledge

NEIL COOPER

I

Those who are involved in education are engaged in the acquisition and transmission of knowledge. But what is this knowledge which is being so acquired and transmitted and which is advanced with each generation? It is the twofold task of the philosopher to answer this question. The first part of his task is descriptive, it consists in setting out the essential characteristics of knowledge. The second part is both more problematic and more important; it is one of appraisal and evaluation. Each age has its cherished intellectual virtues and ideals. What these are is indicated by the terms of intellectual praise (like 'wit', 'learning' and 'intelligence') current in everyday language. The terms favoured may change from time to time and the ideals enshrined in them may need restatement or defence. My aim in discussing knowledge in this paper is to defend one such ideal and to argue for an ancient epistemological principle which is in danger of being eroded because of the acceleration in the growth of knowledge and in the sheer accumulation of information. This principle urges that we should not merely advance what I shall call '*bare* knowledge' but cultivate an understanding kind of knowledge. The principle was, I believe, implicit in the Greek use of the word *episteme*, but it is unclear whether or not it is implicit in the modern English use of the word 'knowledge'. My thesis is that education ought to be the transmission of understanding-knowledge and that an educated person will properly be one who not only has understanding-knowledge but understands the nature of that knowledge.

II

Let us first examine the concept of knowledge. To have knowledge is, I suggest, to have capacities and being educated consists in the acquisition of capacities. The notion of capacities helps to show the formal unity of knowledge. It is easy enough to believe that *knowing-how-to* (or any use of 'know' with *wh*-interrogatives such as 'who', 'what', 'why', 'which', 'where', 'when' and 'whether'), involves a capacity, but it might be thought implausible to describe knowing by acquaintance or knowing-that as capacities also. Now in the case of knowledge by acquaintance, for me to be said to know Roy Jenkins I must at the very least be able to recognise Roy Jenkins as Roy Jenkins (in ordinary life and language we require also that Mr Jenkins should know me). And being able to recognise Roy Jenkins as Roy Jenkins involves at the very least being capable of giving a correct answer on at least some occasions to the question 'Who is this?', asked about Mr Jenkins or his likeness. So knowing by acquaintance involves being able to give a correct answer to a question. Similarly, knowing-that involves being able to give a correct answer to a question. Knowing *that* the faulty valve caused the explosion entails knowing what caused the explosion and knowing what caused the explosion entails having the capacity to give a correct answer to the question, 'What caused the explosion?'. Therefore knowing that the faulty valve caused the explosion entails having a capacity to give a correct answer to a question. Moreover, knowing that the faulty valve caused the explosion entails knowing whether or not the faulty valve caused the explosion. Indeed, every instance of knowing-that entails knowing-whether, and every instance of knowing-whether entails having a capacity to answer a question correctly. The capacity to answer questions correctly is only a little more than true belief and constitutes what I am calling 'bare knowledge'. Of course, to be able to answer a question correctly does not necessarily mean that one does it solely in words. I cannot know how to swim unless I know that *these* are the movements to make. We cannot say all that we know; we sometimes need to complement our words by action, we need to show, demonstrate, indicate, or illustrate. Consider how somebody teaches a musical instrument. The teacher has at times to say, 'Do it like this' and then he plays himself. Or he may get across his message by using a striking metaphor or a simile. 'Don't play like an elephant, pretend you are a fairy', he may say. Knowing is evidenced and transmitted by showing as well as by saying, and what cannot be said can sometimes be shown.

We regard knowledge as a good; other things being equal, we want it and the more we have of it the better. It is what economists call a 'public good' and so we can share knowledge without thereby diminishing anybody's portion. It is because knowledge is a good and the word 'knowledge' is a value-word that Plato sought the definition of *episteme* as well as that of courage, temperance, beauty and justice. Because knowledge is a good or a value there are different and competing standards or conceptions of knowledge. (Epistemology is, in W. K. Clifford's words, the 'ethics of belief'.) There are, however, limits to the range of admissible standards or conceptions, limits set by the logic of knowledge. The lower bound for conceptions of knowledge-that is true belief-that. Anything less than true belief would be false belief and knowledge logically cannot be *that*. (The possibility, however, of knowledge-that being true 'registration'-that in Jonathan Bennett's sense should be considered.[1]) The upper bound for conceptions of knowledge is incorrigibly or infallibly true belief. Paradoxes are generated when a statement is made about knowledge through applying one standard and the same statement is then covertly re-interpreted with the aid of another standard. Thus if we employ an over-stringent standard of knowledge, we may be led to maintain that there is no such thing as human knowledge, that we do not really *know* anything. On the other hand, if we employ an over-lax standard of knowledge, we may be led to maintain that *all* our true beliefs amount to knowledge, so precluding us from articulating any useful ideal of knowledge and making the word 'knowledge' into a superfluous abbreviation of 'true belief'. Any reasonable standard of knowledge must, therefore, lie between these extremes, the lower bound of merely true belief and the upper bound of infallibly true belief. Similar considerations apply to knowledge-how. If we have sufficiently low or lax standards, the bare performance of certain actions may be regarded as warranting the ascription of knowledge-how. Consider knowing how to fly an aeroplane. To warrant ascription of knowledge-how most of us would, I think, require in the pilot some knowledge of how the plane works. On the other hand, we would regard it as unreasonable to require in the pilot the knowledge necessary in an aircraft designer.

III

Let us turn from the concept of knowledge to that of understanding. It is unfortunate that, perhaps as a reaction to neo-Hegelianism, the concept of understanding has been somewhat narrowly construed by recent theorists. It has been supposed that if we are to avoid obscurantism, understanding must be thought of solely as the understanding of language, of words or symbols, sentences or messages. If an ordinary speaker uses the word otherwise, this is often regarded either as a mere manner of speech or a careless error. Thus Russell remarks in his 'The Philosophy of Logical Atomism'[2]:

> I should like to say about understanding that this phrase is often used mistakenly. People speak of 'understanding the universe' and so on. But, of course, the only thing you can really understand (in the strict sense of the word) is a symbol, and to understand a symbol is to know what it stands for.

A non-linguistic conception of understanding appears impalpable and the cautious philosopher is suspicious of a concept whose meaning can be explained, and even then imperfectly, only by accumulating metaphors. We commonly make a distinction between knowledge which is superficial and knowledge which is deep. Homer's comic hero Margites 'knew many things and knew them all badly' and the famous Greek proverb contrasts the fox who 'knows many things' with the hedgehog who 'knows one big thing'. We combine tactual with visual metaphors to express this distinction. We may touch on a topic, or probe it, or penetrate it 'to the core', we may come to grips with it, grasp or comprehend it more or less deeply or thoroughly; we may perceive something dimly at first and then shed light on it or even illuminate it and obtain insight.

The things we meet with in the world we live in are not disconnected from other things. They are things of a kind or sort. They are parts of wholes or wholes of parts. A whole of parts, like a watch, can be understood in terms of its parts. A part of a wider whole, a spring, say, in a watch or a cog in a wheel, can be understood in terms of the whole of which it is a part, element or constituent. Plato saw this when considering the meaning of *logos* in *Theaetetus* (206e–210a). Where there are structures, there are possibilities of understanding. To understand something, I suggest, is to know how to relate it to its structure or to the structure of which it forms a part, element or constituent. In a chaotic universe there would be no structures other than the laws of chance. The world we live in, because it is not chaotic and so has regularities and structures, permits us to structure it in different ways. Our attempts to structure, classify and categorise may sometimes resemble inventions more closely than discoveries, but they are always restricted by what the world permits. Here by 'the world' I mean not merely the physical world but the social world also, which includes societies, institutions, people, works of art, texts and languages. Language is part of the world and understanding language is not distinct from but is part of understanding the world.

IV

Now that I have indicated the principal features of our present concepts of knowledge and understanding, I am in a position to approach the more difficult question of what our epistemological ideals should be. First, we need to distinguish knowledge which is worthwhile from knowledge which is not. To be able to give the correct answer to a question is not in itself to have worthwhile knowledge. Somebody may be able to give correct answers to questions like 'How many words are there in Hume's *Treatise?*', but such answers would not in normal circumstances be regarded as worthwhile knowledge or part of a worthwhile education. What capacities are considered to constitute worthwhile knowledge depends on one's conception of functioning well. In any community there are certain characteristic activities in which normal adults take part. They acquire food and shelter, they engage in work or leisure, communicate and debate, calculate and measure, engage in sexual activity, bring up children, create and administer institutions, take part in social or religious rituals, travel from place to place, and so on. These activities are for the most part common to every society, although in different societies they may take different forms. Each society has a conception of what is required of a well-functioning adult and a corresponding conception of what fundamental capacities it is necessary to acquire in order to function well and engage in these standard activities. There are two sides of this well-functioning. First, there is the practical side; this consists in managing or coping with one's environment, where the environment is social as well as physical. Second, there is the theoretical side; this consists in making sense of and understanding one's environment. Every system of education subserves one or both of these aims. They are indeed connected, since understanding one's environment enables one to cope with it better, and being able to manage one's environment helps one to understand it and amounts to a kind of practical understanding. It is my contention that education and indeed the whole cognitive enterprise should have both aims. Concentration on the practical aim to the exclusion of the theoretical results in a one-sided education; it produces people adjusted to their actual environment but perhaps not capable of adjusting to a changing or novel environment or of actively shaping their environment to meet new needs. Exclusive concentration on the theoretical aim similarly results in a one-sided education; it produces people who cannot cope with the basic needs of life and are only capable of following Socrates's advice in the *Phaedo* and preparing themselves for the life to come.

Second, it is my contention that genuine knowledge requires something more than true belief or even the capacity to produce correct answers to worthwhile questions, it requires understanding. (I shall concentrate to begin with on the case of knowledge-that because it is more tractable.) Anyone who has a true belief that p, ought, if we are to take a claim to knowledge seriously, to understand the phenomena which p describes, and it is natural as a first attempt to interpret 'understand' here as 'understand-why'. For true belief to amount to knowledge, the possessor must be able to give an account of why he holds this belief rather than some incompatible belief; he must not have arrived at his belief at random, but because he has good reasons or adequate evidence or a satisfactory explanation or a justification (notice how naturally evaluative words make their appearance here).

Now according to a standard interpretation of what is meant by 'understand-why', somebody, A, understands why p (where p is some proposition), if there is a proposition q such that A knows that q and q entails p (where entailment is the converse of deducibility). One can, of course, ask further whether A understands the phenomena which q describes in its turn. If A does, then on this standard interpretation of understanding-why, there will have to be a proposition r such that A knows that r and r entails q, and so the chain of knowledge-with-understanding-why will continue without end. On the other hand, if A does not understand the phenomena which q describes, one may legitimately doubt whether A's understanding of the phenomena which p describes can really be good or deep enough, for the phenomena described by p were understood, according to this account, relative to q. We have a dilemma between becoming involved in an endless chain of understanding-why in which nothing is understood, as it were, in its own right or categorically and being committed to a rock-bottom layer or layers of knowledge in which because it is rock-bottom there is no further understanding-why in prospect. If to understand phenomena is to understand-why, that is, to explain them by deducing them from something more fundamental, then this mode of understanding is not open to us with respect to rock-bottom layers of knowledge; otherwise they would not be rock-bottom. We are, then, faced with an apparent dilemma: Either we have no understanding of the phenomena described in a rock-bottom proposition *or* there are modes of understanding other than by means of deductive explanation. The first horn of this dilemma is unacceptable, for if there is no understanding of the foundations of one's knowledge, it is absurd to claim understanding of what rests on these foundations. We have then to choose the second horn of the dilemma, that there are ways of understanding other than through deductive explanation. Not all understanding is understanding-why. The advantage of recognising this is that it enables us in our cognitive undertakings to adopt a more fallibilist line of approach. We can rest temporarily and provisionally on what we at present take to be rock-bottom layers of knowledge while seeking other ways of understanding. An obstacle to this opening-up of the concept of understanding has been the conventional wisdom which states that the task of the natural sciences is to explain (*erklären*) and the task of the social sciences and humanities is to understand (*verstehen*), where explanation and understanding have been supposed to be not merely distinct but contrasted or opposed. I suggest that this distinction was misconceived in the first place and should have been aborted at an early stage.

Misconceived though it may have been, this single-track theory of understanding which I am seeking to dislodge has been influential in the history of thought. One example of this is in the history of quantum theory. In the first chapter of his work *The Principles of Quantum Mechanics*, Paul Dirac speaks of the Principle of Indeterminacy as not something to be regretted but as 'necessary for a rational theory of the ultimate structure of matter'.[3] A classical explanation of the constitution of matter involves explaining its bulk behaviour in terms of laws of the behaviour of its parts. 'There is', Dirac comments, 'no end to such a procedure, so that we can never arrive at the ultimate structure of matter on these lines.'[4] What is wrong with the classical mode of explanation is that if understanding on one level is dependent on understanding at a lower level, all understanding is *conditional* on understanding at a lower level. But if there is no rock-bottom level, there is no unconditional understanding, and that is why if there is no bottom level in Physics, Dirac maintains, there is no ultimate structure of matter of which we can have a 'rational theory'. Heisenberg's Uncertainty Principle together with von Neumann's Theorem, which states that Quantum Theory as it now stands cannot be deduced from any more fundamental set of propositions involving variables below the quantum-mechanical level, ensure the 'rational theory' which Dirac regards as imperative and sufficient. In more recent years, however, physicists have not remained content with this theory as it is, but have tried to supplement it by effecting a 'natural classification' of fundamental particles as giving a deeper understanding of the phenomena. This seems paradoxical since the intellectual orthodoxy has maintained that sciences have a 'natural-history' or taxonomic stage only in their youth. But being able to discern pattern in apparent disorder, to produce a periodic table, say, is a very considerable intellectual achievement. A taxonomic mode of understanding may be as appropriate in the mature state of a discipline as in its beginnings, although plainly its role and context will be conspicuously different. To reduce a multiplicity to order is to achieve some measure of understanding and it is not obviously a form of understanding-why.

V

There are indeed ways of understanding other than by means of deductive explanation. In the first place, one may, instead of providing a deductive explanation, exhibit deductive *connections*. One may seek understanding of a statement by investigating its logical consequences or by finding logically equivalent formulations for it. This has often been done in investigations into the foundations of mathematics, most notably in the case of the Axiom of Parallels in Euclidean Geometry and more recently in the case of the Axiom of Choice in Set Theory.

Second, there are other kinds of connection, not deductive, which provide us with understanding of a given subject-matter. We can see this if we attend to some of our most elementary modes of understanding, those displayed when we interpret human language, conduct and history, which, of course, includes the history of science. My first example is linguistic and social. When I am introduced to somebody who utters the words 'How do you do?' and I reply 'How do you do?', I understand or interpret what is said not as a function of the component words and their surface syntax, and so as a mutual enquiry about the state of our health, but as an instance of a standard form of greeting among people who have just been introduced for the first time. It is the social and linguistic context of the words and utterances which determine how they are to be understood. One understands what might otherwise appear to be a bizarre exchange of questions in terms of a unifying and coherent social situation of which the words uttered form a part. A second and less trivial example is an historical one from Shakespeare's *Julius Caesar*, Act I, Scene II, where off-stage Caesar three times refuses the crown three times offered him by Mark Antony. Such persistent refusal is puzzling. Why should an ambitious man like Caesar refuse so great an honour so pressingly offered? Shakespeare may have known 'little Latin' but he did know his Roman history. There were at least two good reasons for Caesar's refusing the crown and the title of 'rex' associated with it. The first was that the 'reges', foreign tyrants, had been expelled from Rome over five hundred years before and every Roman citizen was brought up to execrate the name and trappings of a *rex*. For this reason 'the common herd was glad he refus'd the crown'. Second, Caesar was a political realist. He did not need the title of 'rex', for it could have added nothing to his absolute power except an idle name and gratuitous opprobrium. This explanation is confirmed by subsequent events, when the sole ruler of the Roman world became known informally as 'princeps' and formally as 'imperator'. Here knowledge of the context, the historical and dramatic context, enables us to make sense of Caesar's conduct, to grasp, comprehend or understand it. In these linguistic, social and historical examples understanding consists in *connecting* the things to be explained with other matters within a pertinent and unifying context. Understanding in this sense may be thought of as knowing where you are intellectually. To plot my position in intellectual space I need an intellectual origin and co-ordinates. I need to connect what I think I know with other things which I also think I know. What all kinds of understanding have in common is the endeavour to make sense of something in terms of its context, whether that context be inferential, social, historical, literary or linguistic. Notice that in trying to understand understanding I am myself exemplifying what I have been talking about, since I am trying to connect one kind or mode of understanding with others.

Third, an important way of making connections and so of coming to understand phenomena is by the use of analogy. The use of analogies, models, pictures and metaphors is a way of making interconnections perspicuous both in the sciences and in the arts (in the realm of metaphor science and poetry meet). We can learn about the less familiar by analogy with the more familiar or even with the more accessible or tangible. The water pump and the valve were more accessible than the human heart and were therefore useful as models for understanding its workings, at a time when it was not actually possible to observe the human heart at work. Further, a versatile analogy like the hydro-mechanical one, the analogy with fluids, may provide one with new concepts in terms of which hitherto unintelligible phenomena may be understood. Apart from its conspicuous employment in the study of electricity, one thinks of its use by Freud in studying phenomena of the unconscious, as well as its utility in the development of twentieth century ethology as shown in Konrad Lorenz's work on animal behaviour.[5] An apt analogy may help to unify different fields of study. Thus Maxwell was able to unify study of the phenomena of light and electromagnetism because, as he found, the laws of two different sciences may have the same mathematical structure. The finding of an illuminating analogy is not just a discovery, it is a creation. It enables us to restructure our problem situation, perceive new possibilities and so facilitate solutions to intellectual problems. But if the finding of an analogy is a creation, knowledge is not just 'out there' to be discovered. Knowledge is created by the interaction with the world of the human observer, experimenter, thinker. That this is what knowledge is is made clearer by emphasising the connection between knowledge and understanding. The concepts are ours, like grids or nets which we cast over the world. If by their means we misinterpret the world or distort it as when, say, we choose a bizarre projection in map-making, the fault is in us, not in the world. That is why we have to make the attempt to understand our ways of understanding, to understand the conceptual means we have for making sense of the world.

Why analogies are aids to understanding is clear from what I said in Section III. There I said that 'to understand something ... is to know how to relate it to its structure or to the structure of which it forms a part, element or constituent'. Now in some cases the structure is conspicuous, it is forced on our attention by the world, it commands recognition; in others we have to apply to our subject-matter conceptual frameworks of our own devising. These conceptual frameworks are derived from previous experience of the world and are normally a social product. To secure understanding they have to be adequate or appropriate to the subject-matter in question. In the case of analogies we try to understand one object by relating its structure to the similar structure of another object which we already understand.

VI

I have maintained that there are different modes of understanding and that these are essential if we are to have genuine knowledge as opposed to bare knowledge. One kind of understanding may reach a terminus, but it is always appropriate to seek some other mode of understanding. Understanding, whether in the natural sciences or in the social sciences or humanities, involves finding a context which relates or unifies the apparently disparate. We have no reason to suppose that some particular mode of understanding is always and necessarily superior to all others. If one mode is blocked, no rigid law of thought precludes us from investigating another mode. Furthermore, we may find that one mode of understanding complements another like the intersecting beams of two searchlights. Thus a mature mathematical science may be presented in a textbook as if it had sprung full-grown from the head of some intellectual Zeus. Yet one may feel the need for the kind of understanding which a more historical approach might achieve. The subject may be studied with profit in both ways, in a logical order from first principles and in an historical order, so that the student recapitulates in his or her own experience the intellectual development of the discipline in question.

The attempt to understand can be justified not only as a good pursued for its own sake, but also because it is itself a means to the advancement of knowledge. The restructuring of problem-situations to which the attempt to understand leads enables us to make new discoveries. It is because we have already existing bare knowledge that we try to understand; in attempting to understand we may acquire fresh knowledge and this faces us once more with the problem of getting further and deeper understanding. Notice that I have spoken of 'deeper' understanding and that we speak and think of understanding things better, improving, broadening, refining our understanding. *Knowledge* in its bare knowledge-that form seems to be of an all-or-nothing character; either you know that *p* or you do not know that *p*. *Understanding* is more like knowledge-how-to and is a matter of degree. Indeed, this suggests (see Section III) that understanding involves knowledge-how-to, in that it consists in knowing how to structure our knowledge, knowing how to connect bits, items, fragments or pieces of knowledge with one another. A kind of knowledge-how-to, then, has to enter into knowledge-that if it is fully to deserve the title of 'knowledge'. In the words of William Whewell, the 19th century mathematician, scientist and philosopher, 'The facts are known, but they are insulated and unconnected, till the discoverer supplies from his own stores a principle of connexion. The pearls are there, but they will not hang together till some one provides the string'.[6]

VII

I have argued that genuine knowledge must be an understanding kind of knowledge. Genuine education, then, must be the transmission of such understanding-knowledge. Now it is surely the case that some bare knowledge cannot even with ingenuity and good will be converted into understanding-knowledge. It is not just *any* knowledge which is properly transmitted in the process of education. There is an immense amount of bare knowledge which is not worth imparting to anybody. My present home telephone number is only of use while I live in my present home to somebody who may want to contact me; knowledge of it does not help anybody to understand anything, unless perhaps one needed to illustrate how different numbers are allocated to different households in our telephone system. Particular facts are not of interest or importance unless they can be connected with other particular facts or can be used to illustrate general propositions. There have sometimes been complaints that competitors in BBC's 'Mastermind' have not been allowed to show their knowledge of, say, winners of the English FA Cup 1884–1983. Presumably the rationale of 'Mastermind' policy on this matter is that little value should attach solely to mental storage capacity. An educated person is not a master memory but one who knows how to connect the apparently disparate within a pertinent and unifying context. The physical constants *seem* to be isolated and particular facts, but this is deceptive. The facts, for example, about the constant velocities of light and sound are particular but they explain and connect with other facts, for example, why we see lightning before we hear thunder. Again, there are certain historical facts that we think it worthwhile to select, record and pass on to others. Churchill's becoming Prime Minister in 1940 was a particular historical event, important because (i) it symbolised defiance in defeat, and (ii) it in fact led to eventual victory. An 'appreciation' of its 'significance' is necessary if we wish to have an understanding-knowledge of events in Britain from 1940 to 1945.

VIII

Now I contended in Section VI that understanding was a matter of degree. I need, therefore, to indicate, even if only in general terms, what degree of understanding is necessary for genuine knowledge and what degree of understanding we should aim to impart in education. There is a very ancient theory of knowledge which stipulates a stringent standard of understanding. According to what I shall call the 'private-enterprise' theory of knowledge, what is or is not knowledge is dependent on the route the individual follows in arriving at a certain conclusion. On this view, the transmission of true conclusions is not sufficient for the transmission of knowledge. For you to know what I know it is not enough that I should tell you what I know and that you should have complete confidence in my honesty, intelligence and knowledgeableness. You must also either follow or be able to follow the route by means of which I arrived at what I claim to know. Consider two people, Euclid the mathematician and Callimachus the poet. Euclid finds a proof that there are an infinite number of primes ('Euclid's Theorem'). But Callimachus has no head for mathematics and cannot follow the proof, although he understands the last line of the theorem and accepts it on trust, because he 'knows' that Euclid is both honest and intellectually outstanding. Callimachus, we would want to say, has true belief, but he does not *know* that there are an infinite number of primes. On this view, somebody can only have knowledge if he has actually travelled the cognitive route; he alone knows who has verified for himself.

The private-enterprise theory is objectionable on two counts. First, it is unduly restrictive on what we can count as knowledge, for it appears to exclude the considerable body of knowledge which is based on testimony or trust. Second, even if the lone cognitive entrepreneur appears to have verified something for himself, this appearance may be illusory. His very loneness exposes him to sceptical doubts. One way of strengthening the theory would be by admitting co-verification. Other people may verify for themselves that Euclid's proof is valid. The view that emerges from this is of a cognitive community, extended over time and space, each member of which is striving to discover for himself truths which may be collectively owned by all. But nobody can verify for himself all known truths. This is why if we are to combine understanding with co-operation in the advancement of knowledge there has to be a division of labour founded on trust.[7] The move from a purely private-enterprise theory to a collective theory bears some formal analogy to the move from 'going it alone' to collective action in prisoner's dilemma situations. Where the knowledge-situation differs is that the temptation to go it alone is only present when individuals are aiming at originality or priority in discovery, as when Crick and Watson were trying to discover the structure of DNA before Linus Pauling. Plainly this does sometimes operate but the extent and complexity of our present knowledge is such as to restrict the scope for such temptation. The private-enterprise conception is a luxury appropriate only to a primitive stage in *our* advancement of knowledge. The ideal which emerges is of knowledge as a social product, fashioned by members of the knowledge-community extended over time and space. We not only say 'I know' but also 'We know'.

IX

The more thought we give to the relations between knowledge-that and knowledge-how, or between knowledge and understanding, the more interconnection we find there. Thus an understanding kind of knowledge-that consists in knowing *how* to connect apparently diverse items. The kind of connection varies according to the subject-matter. It is part of being an educated person that one aims at the kind of connection appropriate to a given subject-matter. An understanding kind of knowledge in any field consists in knowing what *counts* as understanding in that field. To demand a mathematical proof of an alleged historical fact would betray a misunderstanding of what historical knowledge is. To rest satisfied with empirical evidence for a truth of number-theory would be to manifest a misunderstanding of what mathematical knowledge is. In Aristotle's words[8] '... not to know of what things one should demand demonstration, and of what things one should not, argues want of education'. In learning mathematics or history we learn what kind of route to mathematical or historical knowledge is appropriate. Thus we acʌquire two capacities. The first is the higher-order capacity to acquire knowledge, whether this be knowledge-that or knowledge-how. After a certain stage in a discipline one may progress from being taught to *working in* the discipline in question. One then learns without being taught, for one has acquired the capacity to improve one's own skills. This of course applies as much to the fine arts or literature as it does to the sciences. The second capacity is the capacity to make connections within a discipline, to connect apparently isolated bits of knowledge-that or to generalise or extend a skill from one area to another related to it. A basic understanding involves possessing key concepts which enable us to make such connections or to impose unity on diversity. Such understanding is only going to be worthwhile if the connections are in some sense 'really there' and are not merely reflections of our efforts to think coherently and intelligently about the world.

That our knowledge of the world is expressed in a manner which makes it easy to communicate to others must not be a mere product of our will to simplify the world and to make it understandable. An understanding which is not connected with and based on bare knowledge will only be illusion or wishful thinking. So my thesis that understanding ought to be a necessary component of worthwhile knowledge needs to be accommodated to the interconnectedness of knowledge and understanding. It is a well-entrenched maxim of scientific methodology that we should prefer the simplest theory, explanation, hypothesis, or law compatible with our observations. (Basically, the same rule is applied by the scholar engaged, say, in textual or literary criticism). In trying to get more accurate knowledge about a certain range of phenomena we may find that we have to take into account more and more variables. Yet as the number of variables increases, our understanding or grasp may fail to advance. In such cases we may find it impossible to maximise bare knowledge and understanding simultaneously and so we may be forced, although perhaps only temporarily, to choose between the two. Let us take an example from the development of the Kinetic Theory of Gases. The 'ideal' equation of state for a gas is

$$pv = RT,$$

a theoretical equation related to Boyle's empirical law that at a given temperature the pressure of a gas varies inversely with the temperature. This equation takes no account either of any attractive forces existing

between the gas molecules or of the volume of the molecules
themselves. Van der Waals' equation viz.,

$$(p + \frac{a}{v^2})\ (v - b) = RT$$

is less simple; it contains in addition to the variables p, v and T, two
adjustable constants, a and b, a being related to the attractive forces
of each gas and b to the volume of the molecules themselves. The
greater complexity of *this* equation does not impair our understanding of the phenomena; indeed it enhances it, since the introduction of
a and b is theoretically motivated. If, however, we introduce even
more adjustable constants solely in order to fit the observed phenomena, we arrive at more accurate equations but we gain no new
understanding. Such equations, as L.B. Loeb comments 'serve a
useful purpose in expressing the true behaviour of a gas in a
condensed and serviceable form ...' but 'they ... teach nothing about
the phenomena and do not suggest further investigation'.[9]

One can see a possible line of escape from the difficulty of
maximising bare knowledge and understanding simultaneously. It
involves appealing to the two differing but related purposes of the
cognitive enterprise which I distinguished in Section IV, the theoretical and the practical. From the practical point of view, predictive or
technological success is what is really important and in order to attain
it a perhaps temporary halt to progress in understanding may be a
small price to pay. Bare knowledge is a necessity, understanding a
bonus. From the theoretical point of view, overall understanding is
what is really important and in order to attain it a moderate amount
of inaccuracy and oversimplification may be acceptable. This recognises that there is a real tension between bare knowledge and
understanding. While this tension cannot be removed, it can be
alleviated if we make it our cognitive aim to maximise our understanding only in so far as it does not impede the growth of bare
knowledge. This restatement of our cognitive aim is necessary, for to
seek the greatest accuracy with the greatest understanding is, like
aiming at the greatest happiness of the greatest number, attempting
to maximise two goals at one and the same time, and not surprisingly
such a joint maximisation is elusive. If, as Loeb appears to suggest,
understanding goes along with furthering new investigation and
hence obtaining fresh knowledge, a rational resolution of the tension
between bare knowledge and understanding recognises their inter-

connectedness. An understanding of what knowledge is, that is, a knowledge of epistemology, is thus important for the growth of knowledge.

X

It is a standing danger of any theory of knowledge that it will concentrate on cases of knowledge-that and suppose them to be typical of all knowledge. Partly as a corrective to any imbalance, I wish in conclusion to deal with the kind of knowledge which enables us both to manage and to understand ourselves and others. For want of a better name, I shall call it 'sensibility', although one might use the word 'imagination'. It was James Mill's failure to cultivate sensibility which was responsible for the one-sidedness of the education he gave his son. John Stuart Mill's capacities for responding emotionally either to nature or to art or even to human happiness were as a consequence stunted. Only at the age of twenty after a nervous breakdown did he come to realise how the neglect of feeling and 'the undervaluing of poetry' associated with it had impaired his mental progress. It was through experience of Wordsworth's poetry and also of rural beauty that J. S. Mill was able to come to terms with the emotional side of his nature. By contact with nature, art and literature we can indeed learn how to respond more critically and sensitively to our own experience and how to enter imaginatively into the experience of others. Thus understanding a poem involves not only becoming acquainted with a tradition and a style within which emotions can be expressed (e.g. elegiac or pastoral poetry) but also being able to react appropriately. Acquaintance with the tradition and the style involves recognising the technical means of achieving certain poetic ends. Understanding the poem requires in addition knowing how these technical means are used to express characteristically human emotions. The artist *shows* us how, and here saying and showing combine.

The exercise of one's sensibility in everyday life is something for which art can provide a propaedeutic. The novelist or other artist can educate our capacity for sympathy so that we extend it to include within its ambit others different both in character and situation from ourselves. We all naturally see ourselves from the inside. The difficult thing is to see ourselves objectively, to see ourselves as others see us, to acquire self-knowledge, as it has sometimes been called. Self-knowledge involves the capacity to stand outside the contingencies of one's own personality and situation and can often be learned from literature and in particular from the novel and drama. The author of a novel aims to take up an objective stance outside or above the character's view of his or her situation. The reader can learn from the novelist both *that* this is possible and *how* it is possible. The same capacity can be applied to other individuals. As social creatures we are connected with one another; therefore knowing oneself involves knowing others, and to know oneself in connection with others is to understand both oneself and others. Since men have no alternative but to try and understand each other, such knowledge is vital.

XI

I have argued that understanding does not consist merely in the capacity to produce explanations but in the capacity to make connections of many different kinds. It consists in knowing how to structure our knowledge and is thus necessary if our knowledge is to be worthy of the name. I have in this paper tried to justify an ancient commonplace that the cardinal epistemological virtue is knowledge informed with understanding. The transmission of such understanding-knowledge is and ought to be one of the principal aims of education.

NOTES

1. Jonathan Bennett, *Linguistic Behaviour* (Cambridge, 1976) pp. 46–59.
2. Bertrand Russell, 'The Philosophy of Logical Atomism', in R. C. Marsh (ed.), *Logic and Knowledge* (London, 1956) pp. 204-5.
3. Paul Dirac, *The Principles of Quantum Mechanics*, 2nd edn (Oxford, 1935) p. 4.
4. Ibid, p. 3.
5. Konrad Lorenz, 'The Comparative Method in Studying Innate Behaviour Patterns', *Symposia of the Society for Experimental Biology*, vol. 4 (Cambridge, 1950) pp. 220–68.
6. William Whewell, *The Philosophy of the Inductive Sciences*, ii (London, 1840) p. 214.
7. Cf. Hilary Putnam, 'The Meaning of "Meaning"', *Philosophical Papers*, vol. 2 (Cambridge, 1979) pp. 227–9.
8. Aristotle, *Metaphysics*, Book Γ, 1006a 6.
9. L. B. Loeb, *The Kinetic Theory of Gases* (London, 1934) p. 193.

5 On Having a Mind of One's Own

R. S. DOWNIE

It is common to attach importance to 'having a mind of one's own'. For example, it is sometimes said to be part of education (as distinct from training, indoctrination etc.) that it helps one to have a mind of one's own, enables one to think for oneself etc. Again, we might praise someone by saying that his views are very much his own, that he is 'his own man', that he will 'stick to his guns', that his opinions are striking, distinctive or original. Finally, it is often said to be a mark of moral maturity that a person can make up his own mind on moral questions, can choose his own moral views, and so on. Now these and many similar expressions are easy to accept at a common sense level, but as soon as we look at them more carefully it is not at all clear what, if anything, they mean, or what rather different things they might mean.

Let us take some examples of the difficulties in these ideas. It would seem uncontroversial that having a mind of one's own must include having one's own distinctive beliefs about the world, just as one might have distinctive clothes or furniture. But whereas there is no difficulty about understanding how a person can choose distinctive clothes or furniture, there is a problem about understanding how distinctive beliefs, or indeed any beliefs, can be said to be chosen. Beliefs seem more to be involuntary, forced on us by evidence, and if this is accepted then having a mind of one's own becomes more like having distinctive blue eyes than like having a distinctive style in clothes. There is therefore a problem about the sense in which one's beliefs are 'one's own'. Another problem concerns the question of whether, and if so in what sense, it is a good thing to have a mind or beliefs of one's own. For surely, it might be argued, education must at least be concerned with correcting one's own beliefs about various matters, bringing them into line with those beliefs accepted by the acknowledged experts in the field under discussion. For example, a person may have his own views on the causes of the First World War, but if he studies modern history the chances are that he will abandon his own, perhaps erroneous or one-sided, views on the origins of the war and acquire those which are commonly held by more scholarly historians. How then can it be a good thing to have a 'mind of one's own' in history, or indeed in any other respectable academic discipline? It sounds odd to say 'my science' or 'my history', and the fact that one *can* say 'my philosophy' might just mean that philosophy is not a respectable academic discipline!

In view of these and other problems connected with this important idea of having a mind of one's own it seems worthwhile to try to detach it for a while from its context of common sense acceptability and to put it under the philosophical microscope. In this chapter I therefore intend to consider how far or in what sense it is *possible* to have a mind of one's own, what it *consists in* and how its *justification* is linked with being educated. Finally I shall examine the idea in the context of morality where it is familiar to moral philosophers as the problem of the 'autonomy of the will'.

I

The first distinction I wish to draw is crucial to my whole argument. It is a distinction between *independence of mind* and *individuality of mind*. Independence of mind is shown in the kind of support or justification a person might offer for a belief, rather than in either the way in which the belief is acquired in the first place or in the content of the belief. For it is a contingency how a person acquires a given belief; he may acquire it through experience he has had, or through a book he has read or from an influential teacher. But, however the belief is acquired, a person shows independent-mindedness with respect to it insofar as he continues to hold the belief on evidence or similar considerations. A person may of course acquire a belief as a result of encountering evidence for it, but equally it may be a result of his parent's teaching; nevertheless, he is independent-minded if but only if he makes it his own by basing it on whatever is the appropriate evidence. Again, students listening to a lecture might all become convinced of the truth of a certain proposition. They could all be said to be independent-minded with respect to that belief provided each of them based his belief on the argument and the evidence presented (as distinct from the authority of the lecturer), and despite the fact that in the case of each student the *content* of his belief was the same as that of his fellows. On the other hand, a group (if such exists) of independent-minded, argument-devouring students could not be said to have *individuality of mind* in my sense if they all believed the same; individuality of mind does concern differences in the content of people's beliefs, and is much less concerned with the rational basis of the belief. The beliefs of an independent mind are, or purport to be, well-founded, whereas those of an individual mind are or purport to be distinctive, idiosyncratic or unique. (I have drawn the initial distinction between independence of mind and individuality of mind in terms of beliefs, but, as we shall see, it is also shown in styles of living and morality.) I shall concern myself first with the analysis of the independent mind.

Is independence of mind possible? How far can our thoughts be under our own control? The answer here seems to turn on what aspect of thought we are considering, for thought has three different aspects. Firstly, thinking is an occurrence. Ideas occur to the agent and their occurrence can be explained causally in terms of the agent's brainstates, etc. For example, everyone has had the experience of trying unsuccessfully to remember a name, and then the following day having the name stroll into consciousness unbidden. These thought-occurrences cannot be chosen or controlled by the agent, but rather they are caused to enter his mind by other people (comedians like Frankie Howard use this device) or by external factors or his own past experience. Hence, there is no logical possibility of independence of mind here.

Secondly, thinking is holding a belief *that* something is the case, as one might say, 'I think that it will rain soon.' This kind of thinking again is not something a person may be said to *do*; a person cannot take up a position at will. Moreover, he can be made to think that something is the case by another person. In asserting this I am mainly arguing, not from brainwashing and similar techniques, but rather from a whole range of ordinary cases in which A can make B think p to be the case. For example, producing the evidence for p may be a way of making B think that p is the case. In general it seems true that if the evidence for a proposition is sufficiently strong we may come to believe it without choosing to do so. It may be objected that we speak of 'adopting' or 'accepting' a belief. But 'adopting' or 'accepting' ought not here to be regarded as implying that we have a real choice.

We can, of course, choose to ignore the facts in the sense that we can choose to *do* nothing about them, but we do not seem to be free to choose what to think about the facts.

The objection might here be raised that we speak of people *refusing* to believe some unpleasant fact, and indeed people can themselves say, 'I don't choose to believe that.' Before we allow the objection, however, we should consider further what is going on when we are said to refuse to believe something, for there seem to be three possible situations.

Firstly, we may 'in our heart of hearts' believe all the time, and what we are really refusing to do is to *entertain* the belief, allow it to occupy our conscious mind. Secondly, we may refuse to *acquire* the belief by refusing to consider the evidence for it and keeping our attention fixed on the evidence against it. In both these cases the refusal really concerns thinking as an activity. Thirdly, we may be speaking misleadingly when we say 'I refuse to believe that': the situation may be one better conveyed by 'Despite all the evidence, I still find I don't believe that'. It will be seen that none of these three possibilities really implies the ability to choose not to believe that something is the case. I therefore reject the objection, and assert that we cannot choose our beliefs. The conclusion, then, seems to be that thinking, in the sense of believing that something is the case, is not something under our control.

Finally, thinking is an *activity*, and this the agent *can* control. The possibility of such control is seen in the facts that we can tell someone to think about something or not to think about it, that a person can decide to think about something or not to, and that he can be blameworthy for thinking or failing to think about something. For example, a tutor might request a student to think about a certain problem for his next tutorial, and blame him if he has failed to do so. Or we might say 'We should be thinking soon about where we are going for our holidays this year.' These possibilities are (notoriously) limited, but it is reasonable to say that an agent has some measure of control over his thinking in this sense. Granted then that to some extent there is the possibility of controlling and directing one's thoughts in so far as thinking is an activity, it follows that there is also the *possibility* of independent-mindedness.

We can now develop this point by asking how the activity of thinking should be directed to secure independent-mindedness. What does independent-mindedness *consist in*? The first point here is that we begin to be independent of other people in our thinking to the

extent that we base our beliefs on *evidence* or *argument*, as distinct
from the testimony and authority of others. This sweeping statement
must of course be developed and qualified. Different types of
evidence are needed in different sorts of situations, and sometimes
we ourselves may not be able to state the evidence. For example, if
the matter is very technical we may need to rely on the word of
experts. But even here we can acquire some ability to assess where
expertise is relevant and where it is being abused, as when, say,
members of the medical profession ('a doctor writes ...') pronounce
on matters outside their competence as doctors. We can also assess
someone's title to be regarded as an expert, by asking about his
qualifications or experience, or consulting others in the same business. So even here our beliefs can be grounded in evidence, but
indirectly so.

A second factor which makes us independent-minded is our ability
to understand what we claim to have in our minds. For example,
supposing someone is told that Henry VIII dissolved the monasteries
in 1530. How does he make this statement 'his own'? He would need
to understand the claim in several different senses. Thus, he would
need to understand concepts like 'dissolved' as they apply to monasteries. Again, he would need to understand something of the aims of
Henry VIII in order to follow why what he was told was the case, and
he would need to have some idea of the implications of it all, what it
'amounts to', or what the effects of dissolution were on the course of
history. Understanding in these different senses is clearly something
we can have more or less of, and to the extent that we have it we are
more or less independent-minded.

Thirdly, we are independent-minded to the extent that we are
critical of the evidence or arguments for a belief. We may come to
hold that the evidence is insufficient, or of the wrong kind, or that the
arguments are weak. Instruction in the critical appraisal of appropriate evidence is indeed one of the characteristics common to any sort
of academic discipline.

By way of illustration of what it means to be independent-minded
we can consider the student (familiar to anyone who has lectured to
large first-year classes) who inquires, 'Can we use our own ideas, or
must we just regurgitate the lectures?' The questioner is here
confusing individuality of mind (which I shall shortly discuss) with
independence of mind, and he is further presupposing that if his
examinations or essays make use of material acquired from lectures
then he cannot be showing independence of mind. There may also be

the assumption that it is less worthy to copy from a lecture than from a book, presumably on the grounds that it is easier to listen to a lecture than to read a book. But this is not always true (it depends on the lecturer and the book!) and is in any case irrelevant. The relevant point is that independence of mind can be shown in a student's use of material acquired from a lecture. In so far as the student shows a critical understanding of the arguments or evidence he is *ipso facto* showing independence of mind, even although the content of his answers has come from the lecture.

Granted then that independent-mindedness is possible in that we can direct our thoughts to some extent, and that it consists in directing them to appropriate evidence, in understanding what we claim to believe, and in being critical of these beliefs and their evidence, we can now ask about the relationship between being independent-minded and being educated. There seem to be two possibilities. The first is that the connection is causal, that independent-mindedness 'leads to' or is a factor in creating what we call 'being educated'. To take this line is to see the connection as being contingent – the two ideas of independent-mindedness and educatedness are seen to be independently identifiable and one is taken to be conducive to the other. But this is not plausible. To see someone as educated is to *see him as* being independent-minded (in the sense I have outlined) and to see him as independent-minded is to see him as (to some extent and in one sense) educated. The relationship between the ideas cannot therefore be contingent. We must therefore turn to the second possibility, that the relationship is a logical one. It can be claimed to be part of the definition of educatedness that the educated person should have a mind of his own. If this is correct we can explain the importance we attach to being independent-minded and can justify the pursuit of it. To put it in terms of the processes of education, in helping someone to become independent-minded we are by the same token helping him to become educated. Hence, there is abundant justification for trying to acquire independent-mindedness, and for having a mind of one's own in that sense.

Two qualifications should however be noted. The first is that being independent-minded is only part of being educated; it is a necessary but not a sufficient condition of being educated. The educated person is not just independent-minded, but is for example motivated in a certain way – such as being curious about his world – and he has a certain range of knowledge; and no doubt there are other necessary conditions as well. The second qualification is that if we say that independent-mindedness is part of the definition of being educated we cannot also use the notion of independent-mindedness to justify education! This point is worth stressing because it is a temptation when asked to justify the pursuit of education to say that it is worthwhile because among other merits it leads to independent-mindedness. But this is a circle, and I prefer to make independent-mindedness part of the definition of education rather than to justify education in terms of the acquisition of independence of mind. (There are richer justifications of education.)

II

Let us turn now to the second strand in having a mind of one's own – individuality of mind, or the *difference* between people with respect to their beliefs (or activities). The question of the *possibility* of individuality of mind need not detain us; to the extent that independence of mind was possible through the direction of the activity of thought, so is individuality of mind similarly possible. It is when we consider what individuality of mind *consists in* that we find a contrast with independence of mind, and in general the difference concerns the *contents* of the mind.

In the first place, individuality of mind can consist in an *unusual direction* of interest. The person with the individual mind may know about unusual or less commonly known things, such as Victorian toys, the Grassmarket in the 18th century, the science of John of Norfolk, Persian rugs, the songs of troubadours. ... Secondly, the person of individual mind may have a great *depth of knowledge* on some subjects. He may concentrate, to the point of obsession, on a few or just one subject – in this direction lies the scholar knowing more and more about less and less.

In the case of individuality of mind there are possibilities which do not exist for independence of mind – the former but not the latter can be shown in modes which have nothing to do with evidence or understanding or indeed which are not knowledge-based at all. For example, individuality of mind (but not independence of mind) can be shown in ways of dressing, and indeed in ways of living; a style of life can bear a distinctive signature. The term 'originality' can be used for this third side to individuality, and it is above all in the arts that this kind of individuality is shown, although it is also shown in science or philosophy. Some artists reveal their originality in their ability to make us see the familiar in a new light. For example, Wordsworth and Coleridge in their *Preface* to the *Lyrical Ballads* of 1803 said that in their poetry they intended to remove the film of familiarity which everyday experience spreads over things. The person of individual mind can make us appreciate afresh what we already know. Again, originality can consist in the creation of new ideas, or new styles. For example, Wagner or Schoenberg might be said to be great innovators in music, Galileo and Einstein in science, and Kant and Wittgenstein in philosophy. The interesting point is that whether the creative innovation is in art or science or philosophy the result in each case is the same – the human *imagination* is enriched and we can see the world in fresh ways.

What is the connection between individuality of mind and educatedness? It is certainly not part of the definition of educatedness, for it is neither necessary nor sufficient for educatedness. It is not necessary in that we would not withhold the title of educated from a person because he lacked any or all of the characteristics mentioned above. For example, students graduate in their thousands every year who have no unusual direction in their interests, no particular depth in their knowledge and no particular originality, but yet it would be doctrinaire to say that they are not educated, provided they have some independence of mind. It is not sufficient in that a person might have an extensive knowledge of something (cricketers of the 1920s) but still not be educated. Indeed, it may well be that some obsessive scholar in a university has an individual mind, but is barely educated. The point here is that being educated, while it does not logically require deep knowledge of anything or knowledge of unusual things does logically require some breadth of knowledge, and an active curiosity. Such qualities are sometimes conspicuously lacking in distinguished scholars, as in the historian who far from having a general curiosity about science, art, politics, etc. is not even interested in events six months outwith 'his period'.

To maintain that a person with individuality of mind is not for that reason educated is not to say that he is not highly desirable in other ways. Educatedness is only one kind of good and should be balanced against the obsessive scholar or the creative artist or the performer who devotes his life to practising an instrument. These too are good lives. The problem is that while educatedness is logically consistent with individuality of mind it is psychologically and practically difficult to combine the two. The explanation is that to be educated, as I have asserted, requires as a necessary condition a certain breadth of interest. Now breadth of interest is logically compatible with the conditions of individuality, but empirically the two do not go easily together, and it is difficult and unusual for a person to have both. Centres of higher education are designed to produce independence of mind, but are poor at producing individuality of mind. The latter claim is perhaps an unfair way of putting the point since they do not set out to produce individuality of mind. Nevertheless, there is a certain grey uniformity about what comes out of universities.

If individuality of mind cannot be justified as being part of the definition of educatedness how can it be justified, if at all? There are two sorts of justification, one in terms of self-development and the other in terms of the plural and varied society. The source for both forms of justification here is J. S. Mill's Essay *On Liberty*. Mill tells us that the end of man is 'the highest and most harmonious development of his powers to a complete and consistent whole'.[1] These powers are developed by pursuing ends which are rich and complex and therefore suitable for bringing out the potentialities within us. It is true that many people will prefer pushpin to poetry but (Mill would say) they are dull people whose individuality has never been developed. As Mill himself puts it, 'It really is of importance not only what men do but also what manner of men they are that do it'.[2] There is a second and complementary strand to Mill's thinking here. He stresses the importance of the conscious and choiceful pursuit of objectives. On this view the stress is on 'being oneself' as opposed to 'conforming to custom'. A custom may be a good one but 'to conform to custom merely *as* custom does not educate or develop [in a person] any of the qualities which are the distinctive endowment of a human being'. Mill seems here to equate self-development with 'being original', but this is intelligible if we assume that no two people are quite alike, so that to be oneself is to be not quite anyone else, and in this sense to be 'original' or to have individuality of mind. The cultivation of individuality of mind is to be justified then in that it is a necessary condition of self-development.

At this point it might be objected that one frequently offered justification of educatedness (which has independent-mindedness as a necessary component) is that it too leads to self-development. Now this may be true, but it is not an objection to justifying individuality in terms of self-development; for I have not asserted that there is a logical incompatibility between individuality of mind and independence of mind, but only that it is difficult to combine the cultivation of both. We might expand this point by distinguishing between the 'generic' human self or the 'distinctive endowment of a human being' (to use Mill's phrase) and the 'idiosyncratic' self. To be educated is to have achieved some development of distinctive human endowments – which Mill lists as the 'human faculties of perception, judgment, discriminative feeling, mental activity, and even moral preference which are exercised only in making a choice'.[3] In other words, to be educated is to have developed the generic self, those qualities which are common to us all. Individuality of mind by contrast is concerned with the development of at least some of those qualities and interests which are peculiar to a given person. Now the development of these idiosyncratic qualities will make use of the generic features of the human endowment, the features on Mill's list, but will turn these 'features' in a distinctive direction. Independence of mind and individuality of mind will both therefore find their justification in self-development, but in different ways.

Individuality of mind (like independence of mind and the larger concept of educatedness) can also be given justification in terms of social utility. It is from the variety of interests or even the conflict of interests to which individuality of mind gives rise that social progress develops. Adventures in ideas and in forms of life are necessary if a society is not to stagnate, and it is those with individuality of mind that are most likely to have such adventures.

III

Is there anything corresponding to independence of mind and individuality of mind in the sphere of morality? Take independence of mind. A person is sometimes said to have a capacity to 'think what he likes on moral matters', 'make up his own mind on moral issues', 'decide for himself what he ought to do', 'choose his own moral position' etc. From these expressions it seems that there is independence of mind on moral matters, but the idea is not without complexity so once again I shall ask the three questions: how is it possible? what does it consist in? how can it be justified?

Independence of mind in moral thinking is *possible* in the same way and to the extent that any sort of independent thinking is possible. I argued that in one sense thinking is an activity, and as such we can control it, as we can control our other activities. The same is true of thinking on moral matters. To this extent independence of mind on moral matters is possible. What does it consist in? There are three strands to it.

Firstly, a moral agent must be independent-minded in that he cannot hand over his entire moral thinking to any authority such as a church, a state or parents. This is really a logical thesis, for it rests on the fact that there is one basic question which the authority logically cannot answer: is it right to take this body as one's authority on moral matters? Of course, a man may not raise such a question explicitly, but in so far as he treats a body *as* a moral authority – 'I ought to do this because the Church commands it' – he is presupposing an affirmative answer to the basic question. Notice that this thesis applies, not only to our relationship with authorities such as Church, State or parents, but also to our situation as regards vaguer considerations which we may come to regard as authoritative, such as 'the done thing', 'what I always do', 'what my station in life demands', etc.

The second strand in this complex idea takes the form of a *moral doctrine*: that a person has a moral right to think out for himself what he ought to do, and need not just accept what others tell him. This is a central tenet of Liberal-Protestantism, and it must be carefully distinguished from the first strand. The first strand was that a man logically cannot but think for himself to a minimal degree on moral matters; the second is that a man has a moral right to do all his own thinking on moral matters.

It may be objected that it does not make sense to speak of a man's right not to accept what others tell him. For if a man believes that some body (for example, the Catholic Church) is a valid authority on moral matters, he cannot choose to hold that he ought not to obey it (at least on the view that we cannot choose a moral position).

This objection, however, rests on a confusion. The right to think out a moral position for oneself is a right to perform the *activity* of thinking with regard to moral matters, including the right to sift the claims of a body to be a moral authority. As we saw, thinking in this sense is something which a man can choose to do or not do. It is the *result* of this process which is not under the agent's control. For example, he may as a result of exercising his right come to regard a certain body as authoritative in moral matters – perhaps entirely against his inclinations. We can interpret this result as the acquisition of either a new belief or a new attitude. But in either case, he cannot now choose to hold that he ought not to obey the authority in question. But he can choose to continue thinking about its credentials – though such an activity may be considered disloyal by the authority to which he now subscribes.

How can we further characterise the right to think out our moral positions? We may say that it comprises both a right of action and a right of recipience.[4] It is a right of *action* in that the agent is held not to be acting wrongly – showing undue presumption or folly, for example – in thinking for himself. It is a right of *recipience* in that others have a duty not to interfere with the process by undue pressure or propaganda or by showing lack of respect for the conclusions reached.

But although this second side to moral independence demands respect for others' moral conclusions, it does not imply that the individual's own moral thinking is immune from error – though in practice it has often been associated with a belief in an infallible conscience or inspiration. Nor does it even imply that one man's moral thinking is likely to be as good as another's. Rather the notion seems to be that the thinking as such is a valuable human activity, and that convictions which are worked for are more deeply held than those which are accepted without questioning. Seen in this way thinking out one's moral positions for oneself emerges as not just a right but as a duty.

The third strand in the idea of moral independence, like the second, is a moral doctrine; that a man has a right to be judged in terms largely of his *own* moral standards rather than those of other people. We may express this right by saying that moral agents possess a measure of 'judicial independence'. The doctrine of judicial independence depends, not on any belief in individual infallibility, but rather on the notion that if a man does what *he* sincerely considers to be right he has acted dutifully and in good faith, and his blameworthiness is therefore limited. But the right of judicial independence is restricted by the fact that questions of the blameworthiness of the agent are not always, or completely, independent of the views of others. We do blame people for actions which they believed to be right if we feel that their error (as we see it) is their own fault. And this is quite often the case, as when we attribute the error to a lack of perceptiveness which everyone can and should acquire, or a failure to exercise the right to think for oneself which I have just described. Nevertheless, it remains true that blameworthiness is to some extent independent of the views of other people, and to that extent judicial independence is a genuine component in the complex idea of moral independence and may be added to the other two components.

How can we justify this doctrine of moral independence of mind? The answer is that it is a logically necessary component of the liberal attitude. Liberalism by definition allows the right to make up one's own mind on moral questions and restricts blameworthiness by referrring to the agent's own moral standards (as in conscientious objection). This justification of course assumes that we accept liberalism, but something must be assumed if progress is to be made in developing a set of ideas.

Is there anything corresponding to individuality of mind in the sphere of morality? In so far as morality is a social phenomenon the possibility of individuality of mind must be restricted. If moral duties stem from social rules which exist for the benefit of a society as a whole and apply impersonally to all of us then the possibility of moral individuality must be restricted. But it still exists. For example, even although rules apply to all alike there are more or less imaginative ways of carrying out one's duties, and those ways can show individuality. Again, not all conduct is rule-bound and some people have much more of an insight into the needs of their neighbours or their own weaknesses than others do. Moral individuality is shown here. The point here is easiest brought out if we consider the saints and heroes of the moral life, who all reveal a different style of life. For example, John Hampden, St. Francis, etc., all revealed a different sort of moral individuality related no doubt to non-moral gifts and idiosyncrasies. Morally good people of one's own acquaintance reveal in more humble ways this same diversity of approach to the moral life.

Indeed, this side to morality is the one which many people regard as making up the whole of morality. Thus, it is not uncommon for people to think of morality as radically subjective, to take the view that there are as many different moralities as there are people holding them. It would then seem that *all* moral choice shows individuality of mind since all moral choice is just the expression of subjective taste. Moreover, some philosophers might take it further and argue that unless moral choice reflects one's individuality it is mere conformity to convention.

This position is confused, in that it is based on an exaggeration and a misinterpretation. It exaggerates the extent to which there is moral diversity in a given society. Obviously people in our own society disagree over many matters – the use of surrogate mothers, the crossing of picket lines, private health care and so on – but there is nevertheless a broad consensus on moral matters. And this is not just a contingency. For whatever else morality is, it is at least a system of social organisation, and there must (causally) be a reasonable consensus on the broad outline of this organisation otherwise the society will collapse. Now, whereas there are occasionally moral reformers who criticise important features of a given social organisation, moral individuality must normally be shown within the broad framework, otherwise it is deleterious to the fabric of society.

The position also misinterprets a truth. The truth is that, as we have seen, moral *independence* of mind requires of us that we think out for ourselves our own moral positions. But it does not follow from this that each person will have different moral beliefs, or will choose to act differently from his fellows. It is arguable that Existentialists were guilty of this confusion. Moving from the plausible premise that moral authenticity is shown in moral independence of mind – the agonising thinking out for oneself of what one ought to do, and in the conscious choice of action or policy – they reached the implausible conclusion that authenticity is shown in choosing against the morals of one's society. But there is no reason why it should be morally better, even from an Existentialist point of view, to choose against the prevailing customs of one's society than to choose with them. Certainly there is always scope for innovation in morality, for originality in one's style of life, but moral individuality can never be the whole of morality.

But, granted that moral individuality does have an important place in morality of the kind I have mentioned, it is not difficult to make explicit its justification. It should be encouraged in moral education and in ordinary life for the same reason as non-moral individuality of mind should be encouraged – it develops our creativity and our uniqueness as distinctive selves, and is both partly conducive to and also partly constitutive of a rich and varied society.

NOTES

1. J. S. Mill, *On Liberty*, (London: Collins, Fontana Library, ed. by Mary Warnock, 1962), ch. 3.
2. Mill, op. cit., ch. 3, p. 188.
3. Mill, op. cit., ch. 3. p. 187.
4. For the distinction between rights of action and rights of recipience see D. D. Raphael 'Human Rights, Old and New', in D. D. Raphael (ed.), *Political Theory and the Rights of Man* (London: Macmillan, 1967).

6 Humanistic Education: Some Philosophical Considerations

G. H. R. PARKINSON

In this chapter, I propose to discuss some of the ideas contained in Richard Rorty's recent book.[1] The book has been widely praised, and not without reason. The author goes for big issues, such as the nature of the mind and of philosophy itself, and he tackles them in an exciting way. More than this, he is free from the parochialism of which philosophers of the English-speaking world are often accused. He is well-versed (for example) in Quine, Davidson and Kuhn, but he is equally at home with the views of continental philosophers such as Sartre, Gadamer, Derrida and Heidegger. What makes the book relevant to the philosophy of education is its defence of what Rorty calls[2] 'the humanist tradition in education'. Rorty does not define this term, but it is clear from the course of his argument that he is concerned to defend, not just classical education[3] but literary culture in general, 'literacy' as opposed to 'numeracy'.

Rorty's defence of humanistic education does not constitute a major part of his book. But it is closely connected with some of his most distinctive philosophical views, so that in discussing his philosophy of education one is led to discuss the very bases of his philosophy as a whole. To be more precise, one is led to discuss Rorty's views about the nature of knowledge, for it is these views which form the basis of his defence of humanistic education. But an assessment of Rorty's defence must do more than examine his views about knowledge. Rorty offers a *philosophical* defence of humanistic education; it is necessary, therefore, to look also at his views about the nature of philosophy. These views will be my first concern.

Kant, thinks Rorty, made a profound mistake in trying to put philosophy on the secure path of a science. It was not that the idea was good and the execution faulty; rather, the whole enterprise was misconceived.[4] If this were an error peculiar to Kant, the damage would not be great. But the same error is to be found in many other philosophers: in Russell, Carnap, and indeed in most Anglo-Saxon philosophers.[5] This error about the nature of philosophy has its roots in a false picture of the nature of knowledge and of rationality: the picture of a mirror of nature.

Here we meet a problem of interpretation: namely, just what Rorty means by a 'mirror of nature'. He appears to use the term in two senses, one being narrower than the other. In the narrow sense, the notion of a mirror goes with the notion of the representation of an object. It goes with the notion that to talk about objective knowledge is to talk about accurate representation,[6] accurate representation of the essences of things. These essences, it is supposed, are objectively *there*,[7] and knowledge is a matter of the undistorted reflection of such essences. The notion of rationality is viewed in the same way. To argue rationally, according to this version of the 'mirror of nature' view, consists in 'finding the correct vocabulary for representing essence'.[8]

Now, I have just mentioned Kant as one of the targets of Rorty's attacks, and it springs to mind that the view of knowledge just described is precisely the one that the *Critique of Pure Reason* is meant to overthrow. For Kant, knowledge does not conform to objects; rather, objects conform to the conditions of our knowledge. However, there is a wider sense of 'mirror of nature' which can include Kant. Rorty says that his book is written in opposition to 'the notion that there is a permanent neutral framework whose "structure" philosophy can display'; the notion that 'the objects to be confronted by the mind, or the rules which constrain inquiry, are common to all discourse, or at least to every discourse on a given topic'.[9] The idea of rules that are common to every discourse on a given topic is one to which Kant would have subscribed; his categories are surely rules of this sort, or at any rate closely related to them.[10] As to the idea that philosophy is concerned with essences, which is part of the narrower concept of a mirror of nature, this can easily be accommodated within the wider concept. What one has to do is to take these essences, not as objectively 'out there' but as imposed by the mind, as a Kantian category is imposed.

It seems, then, that the wider sense of the term 'mirror of nature' is the one that Rorty requires: the sense in which the 'permanent neutral framework', whose existence is required by knowledge and by rational thought in general, is one of rules rather than of 'objects to be confronted by the mind'. But the passage just quoted[11] shows that Rorty does not distinguish clearly between the two senses of a 'mirror of nature', and I will argue later that this ambiguity in the term is damaging to his position as a whole.

Although Rorty thinks that many philosophers are mistaken about the nature of their subject, he does not propose that philosophy shall be abandoned; his aim is the reform of philosophy, not its abolition. The kind of philosophy that he advocates can be introduced by way of a question that students of philosophy sometimes put to their teachers. 'Why', these students say, 'should we bother with the history of philosophy? We want to know about the good and the true; we do not want to know what people thought about these topics hundreds of years ago.' Rorty would answer[12] that there is no division of labour between the philosopher and the historian. 'Cultural anthropology (in a large sense which includes intellectual history) is all we need'.[13] Briefly, his thesis is that philosophers who try to find a 'permanent and neutral framework' for rational thought merely 'eternalise a certain contemporary language-game, social practice, or self-image'.[14] What such philosophers call 'rationality' is simply 'the philosophical dogmas of the day'.[15] In defence of this view, Rorty makes use of the ideas of Kuhn, whose book[16] has proved to be one of the most important works on the philosophy of science published in recent years. Rorty takes Kuhn's view that certain scientific theories are not 'commensurable' and extends it to cover, not just theories within science, but the relations between scientific discourse as a whole and other types of discourse.

Rorty explains[17] that by 'commensurable' he means 'able to be brought under a set of rules which will tell us how rational agreement can be reached on what would settle the issue on every point where statements seem to conflict.' The key notion, then, is that of rules for securing rational agreement. Rorty notes[18] that in discussions of Kuhn, the term 'commensurable' often has a different sense, namely that of 'assigning the same meaning to terms'. By taking the word 'commensurable' in the way that he does, Rorty is able to escape an objection brought against Kuhn: namely, that on Kuhn's view we simply *cannot understand* the sentences uttered by those whose terms are not commensurable with ours.[19] On Rorty's view, we can understand the sentences that such people utter; what makes these sentences incommensurable with ours is a difference in the rules used for securing rational agreement. The geocentric controversy may serve as an illustration of incommensurability. Rorty would say that Galileo on the one hand, and the representatives of the Roman Catholic church on the other, meant the same by the terms that we translate as 'the sun', 'the earth' and 'moves round'. But the rules that Galileo and his fellow-Copernicans followed in securing rational agreement led them to accept the truth of 'The earth moves round the sun', whereas the different rules followed by Galileo's opponents led them to reject it as false.

Rorty, then, links commensurability with the possibility of rational agreement. But what, in his view, makes agreement rational? Rorty shows by implication that such agreement cannot be enforced; he remarks that it is a common (and, he implies, unjust) reaction to Kuhn that he is advocating the use of force rather than persuasion.[20] Rational agreement, then, is reached by means of persuasion; but more has to be said. One can be persuaded to accept certain views by means of (for example) someone's fiery oratory, but this does not make one's agreement with the orator *rational*. Rational agreement, one might suppose, is where one is persuaded by argument. But argument presupposes the acceptance of rules; and what makes these rules binding? Rorty's answer is in effect that what constitutes rationality is just what is accepted as rational by a given group of people at a given time.

He illustrates his point[21] by the controversy that I have just mentioned: that between Galileo on the one hand and the anti-Copernicans, whose spokesman was Cardinal Bellarmine, on the other. Was Bellarmine 'illogical or unscientific' in basing his belief in the geocentric theory on the authority of the Bible (or to be more exact, on the Bible as interpreted by the Catholic church)? We have to tread carefully here.

(1) There is one sense in which Bellarmine's defence of the geocentric theory might be represented as perfectly logical, perfectly rational; but this sense is not the one that Rorty has in mind. Let us suppose[22] that to shake the authority of the Bible is to shake the authority of the Church, and of the cultural and perhaps also the political structure of Europe in general. Then it is rational for those who want to preserve this structure to silence those whose work will shake the authority of the Bible. That this is not the sort of rationality that Rorty has in mind is clear from the fact

that *how* such people are silenced does not matter; if force is necessary, then it would be rational to use force. Rorty, however, has explained that the agreement that he is concerned with is not one that is based on force. For him, the question is: will Bellarmine's argument for the geocentric theory stand up *as an argument*?

(2) Well, why should it not? As Rorty asks, 'What determines that Scripture is *not* an excellent source of evidence for the way the heavens are set up?'.[23] Rorty's answer is that our views about what constitutes good argument for the structure of the heavens are Galileo's views; 'Galileo, so to speak, won the argument'.[24] The phrase 'so to speak' may indicate Rorty's awareness of the fact that he is not speaking accurately here. To talk of winning an argument is to imply that there is common ground between the contestants, that they accept common standards of rationality – and this is supposed *not* to hold between Galileo and Bellarmine. Elsewhere, Rorty says that we are 'the heirs of three hundred years of rhetoric about the importance of distinguishing sharply between science and religion',[25] and this seems to state his view more accurately. Galileo won, we might say, not an argument but a debate, and he won the debate because his rhetoric was the more effective. This is not to say that Rorty sides with Bellarmine. Speaking of the three hundred years of rhetoric that I have just mentioned, he says[26] 'This rhetoric has formed the culture of Europe. It made us what we are today. ... But to proclaim our loyalty to these distinctions [between science and religion, for example] is not to say that there are "objective" and "rational" standards for adopting them.'

This is why I said that, for Rorty, rationality is just what is accepted as rational by a given group of people at a given time. 'In 1550 a certain set of considerations was relevant to "rational" views on astronomy, and by 1750 a largely different set of considerations was relevant'.[27] All this is a full-blooded relativism; we could call it a *cultural* relativism, the implication being that (for example) Galileo and Bellarmine belonged to different cultures. Now, it is well-known that relativism is faced with problems of self-reference; that is, that relativists get into difficulties when their own views are applied to them. One of the philosophers of whom Rorty approves is Quine,[28] so it will be apposite to quote Quine's formulation of the relativist's dilemma. 'Truth, says the cultural relativist, is culture-bound. But if it were, then he, within his own culture, ought to see his own culture-bound truth as absolute. He cannot proclaim cultural relativism without rising above it, and he cannot rise above it without giving it up'.[29]

Rorty tries to find an answer to this line of argument. The trouble, as I have said, springs from self-reference; it arises when claims that knowledge or truth are relative are themselves proclaimed as known, or as the truth. But what if there is a philosophy that does not claim to be the truth? This, it seems to me, is the essence of the kind of philosophy that Rorty wants to defend; a 'philosophy without mirrors', as he calls it.[30] At this point, Rorty turns to continental philosophy for assistance. He ranges himself alongside Gadamer and the views about 'hermeneutics' that are associated with him. In his book[31] Gadamer says that 'The hermeneutics developed here is not ... a methodology of the human sciences, but an attempt to understand what the human sciences truly are, beyond their methodological self-consciousness, and what connects them with the totality of our experience of the world'. Rorty interprets this as follows. There is, he says, a 'classic picture' of man as a being whose essence it is to discover essences, 'to mirror accurately ... the universe around us'[32] Gadamer's achievement is to have redescribed man in such a way as 'to place the classic picture within a larger one, and thus to "distance" the standard philosophical problematic rather than offer a set of solutions to it'.[33] What, then, is the 'larger picture' of man that Gadamer offers? According to Rorty[34] one of Gadamer's virtues is his ability to do justice to the romantic notion of man as self-creative. 'He does this by substituting the notion of *Bildung* (education, self-formation) for that of "knowledge" as the goal of thinking'. This notion of self-formation through reading, talking and writing is linked by Rorty with the notion of self-expression. He says[35] that 'Getting the facts right (about atoms and the void, or about the history of Europe) is merely propaedeutic to finding a new and more interesting way of expressing ourselves, and thus of coping with the world'. This last sentence deserves careful examination.

(a) 'Getting the facts right.' It would be wrong to suppose that Rorty has no place for the notion of objectivity, whether in the natural sciences ('atoms and the void') or in what Gadamer calls 'the human sciences' ('the history of Europe'). But he insists that objectivity has to be seen[36] as 'conformity to the norms of justification (for assertions and for actions) that we find about us'. Here the phrase 'that we find about us' is crucial. The norms of justification are not fixed and eternal; they are the norms of a given epoch, a given culture.

(b) It emerges from what has been said in (a) that Rorty is not opposed to the natural sciences; they have a place within *Bildung*. But, as he makes clear later,[37] they provide only 'some, among many, ways of describing ourselves'. He is opposed, not to science, but to scientism – meaning by this the thesis that the totality of what can be said is constituted by what can be said in the language of the natural sciences.[38]

(c) At the same time, getting the facts right is not an end in itself; it is propaedeutic to something else.

(d) This end is described as 'finding a new and more interesting way of expressing ourselves', and ways of expressing ourselves are ways of 'coping with the world'. The notion of 'coping' is an important one in Rorty's thought. It seems to appear first in chapter 6, section 2, where Rorty is discussing the question of what made Newton a better physicist than Aristotle. He was better, Rorty says,[39] 'not because his words better corresponded to reality but simply because Newton made us better able to cope'. Then, at the end of chapter 7, we are told[40] that 'Hermeneutics is not "another way of knowing" ... it is better seen as another way of coping'. This brings out the pragmatist strand in Rorty's thought. To cope is to deal with successfully[41]; that is, the ways of self-expression that Rorty finds interesting are the ones that *work*.

Rorty proposes to render Gadamer's term *Bildung* by the word 'edification'; edification, then, is the project of finding 'new, better, more interesting, more fruitful ways of speaking',[42] and the philosophers whose project this is may be termed 'edifying philosophers'.[43] We come now to the crucial point. Does this view of the nature of philosophy enable Rorty to answer the argument against relativism that I cited from Quine? Rorty has said that philosophy must be something other than knowledge; no philosopher can justifiably claim to possess the objective truth, because what is counted as objective truth is culture-relative. To this the objection was: if everything that is claimed to be true is culture-relative, what reason have we to accept Rorty's views as true? There is a further problem for Rorty, which is linked with his pragmatism. The interesting views, he says, are those which enable us to cope. But how do we *know* that we are coping? Rorty does not seem even to try to answer the second question, but he does try to answer the first. I suggested earlier that his answer is in essence that there is a type of philosophy that does not claim to be the truth. We have just seen what this philosophy is: it is 'edifying philosophy'. 'The notion of an edifying philosopher', Rorty remarks,[44] 'is ... a paradox. The problem for àn edifying philosopher is that *qua* philosopher he is in the business of offering arguments, whereas he would like simply to offer another set of terms, *without* saying that these terms are the new-found accurate representations of essences (e.g. of the essence of "philosophy" itself) ... [Edifying philosophers] refuse to present themselves as having found out any objective truth'.

The problem is, whether this view of the nature of philosophy will stand up to criticism. Let us take as an example one of the things said by an edifying philosopher, namely by Rorty himself. I mentioned early in this paper that Rorty claims[45] that Kant was wrong in trying to put philosophy on the secure path of a science. Are we to suppose that what Rorty told us there is not true? Rorty might perhaps reply, 'Not true, but interesting and useful'. But then we would counter with, 'But is it *true* that it's interesting and useful?' In fact, Rorty's answer is different. He concentrates on what I have called the 'narrow' sense of the term 'mirror of nature', explaining that when he says that he is not concerned with objective truth, he means only that he is not concerned to offer accurate representations of how things are.[46] Edifying philosophers, he says,[47] do not have a view about having views, by which he means that we are to get rid of visual metaphors, and in particular the metaphor of mirroring, when we talk about knowledge and truth. But this misses the whole point of the basic objection to a cultural relativism such as Rorty's. This *ignoratio elenchi* springs from Rorty's failure to grasp the ambiguity in his own term, 'mirror of nature'. The argument against Rorty is not that he is really using a visual metaphor; it is that he claims to *know*, whilst saying that every claim to knowledge is culture-relative. In other words, the objection does not involve any specific view about the nature of knowledge; it certainly is not restricted to what I have called the 'narrow' sense of the term 'mirror of nature', but is equally telling against the wider sense.

The only way out of Rorty's difficulties, it seems, is for him to make some concessions: to grant that there are *some* objective truths that can be known, even if most alleged items of knowledge are culturally relative. Let us assume that he would accept this, and ask:

what is the relevance of Rorty's views about 'edification' to humanistic education? The beginnings of an answer are to be found in the sentence that follows the one analysed in detail above ('Getting the facts right ... etc.'). This says that 'From the educational, as opposed to the epistemological or the technological point of view, the way things are said is more important than the possession of truths'. In a note to this, Rorty remarks[48] that 'The contrast here is the same as that involved in the traditional quarrel between "classical" education and "scientific" education. ... More generally, it can be seen as an aspect of the quarrel between poetry (which cannot be omitted from the former sort of education) and philosophy (which, when conceiving of itself as super-science, would like to become foundational to the latter sort of education)'.

When Rorty speaks of the quarrel between poetry and philosophy (he means, of course, philosophy that claims to provide knowledge of essences) he may have in mind the etymology of the word 'poetry', i.e. its link with poiēsis, making. The antithesis is really between the creative activities of the human being and those in which we respond to what is outside us in a more or less mechanical fashion. Similarly, his contrast between 'the way things are said' and 'the possession of truths' is a contrast between those utterances which are forms of self-expression and those which are not. His thesis, then, amounts to this: that classical (or, more generally, humanistic) education aims at creativity and self-expression, whereas scientific education aims at a mere accumulation of knowledge.

But Rorty is not concerned simply to explore the differences between humanistic and scientific education; he also implies that the former is the better sort of education. For this, he seems to have two chief arguments. First, scientific education presupposes that there *is* knowledge that is objective and fixed for all time, and this presupposition is false. I have argued that Rorty will have to accept *some* objective truths, but he would probably reply that these are far fewer than those that are taught in science courses as the known truth. Humanistic education, on the other hand, does not presuppose that there is such knowledge. It is concerned, not with knowledge of facts, but with *making* – more specifically, with the self-creation of human beings.

The second argument is related to the first. Rorty quotes with approval Gadamer's views about the relations between *Bildung* and an awareness of cultural relativity. He expresses Gadamer's views by saying[49] that if we are to give sense to the notion of *Bildung*, 'we need a sense of the relativity of descriptive vocabularies to periods, traditions, and historical accidents. This is what the humanist tradition in education does, and what training in the results of the national sciences cannot do'. He adds that by themselves, the natural sciences 'leave us convinced that we know both what we are and what we can do'. A humanistic education, he implies, is free from arrogant delusions of this kind.

A critic of Rorty might object that his account of scientific education is a mere caricature. It is not the case (the critic might say) that such an education consists exclusively in 'training in the results of the natural sciences'. Of course it involves such training; to adapt Newton's famous remark, it is mere foolishness to refuse to stand on the shoulders of the giants who have preceded us. But a scientific education should also enable the student to enlarge the sciences, and this extension of the realm of scientific knowledge is an activity of the imagination. The scientist can be as creative as the humanist.[50] Nor is it correct to say that the natural sciences leave us convinced that we know what we are and what we may be. Some scientists may be dogmatists of this kind, but there is nothing in natural science that entails such dogmatism.

It is not clear, from what is said in *Philosophy and the Mirror of Nature*, how Rorty would answer this. Perhaps he might reply that it is sufficient for his purposes if a scientific education *tends towards* narrowness and dogmatism of the kind that I have described; it *tends to* make us think that we have the answers to many fundamental questions, and such tendencies are not present in humanistic education. But leaving aside the fairness, or unfairness, of Rorty's account of scientific education, will his defence of humanistic education hold water? His defence of such education, and indeed of *Bildung* in general, rests on a view of man – a view of man as self-creative.[51] But this view, like all other such views, is surely subject to Rorty's cultural relativism. Rorty must in consistency say that it makes no sense to ask whether or not this picture of man is true; it just *is* the picture that certain people have, or have had. We now ask why Rorty should prefer this picture to others, such as the picture of man as a being which seeks to mirror essences. Rorty's reply will take us further into his views about the nature of philosophy.

We must first note[52] that the view of man as self-creative, and the view of man as a being which tries to mirror essences, are what Rorty calls 'incommensurable'; the humanist and the scientist have different methods of securing rational agreement. Now Rorty argues that it is precisely for such situations that we need edifying (or, as he also calls it, 'hermeneutic') philosophy.[53] Hermeneutic philosophers do not try to prove that one side is right and the other wrong; in Rorty's words, they replace confrontation by conversation.[54] This of itself tells us little; we want to know what such conversation is like. Is it, for example, like the conversation that one gets in Plato's dialogues, where Socrates exposes the muddled views of his opponents? I think that Rorty's official answer must be 'No'; critical conversation of a Socratic type, he would say, presupposes commensurable discourse, and edifying philosophy comes in where the forms of discourse are not commensurable. What Rorty means by edifying conversation is shown by a passage[55] in which he gives his answer to the very problem that we have raised: namely, the attitude of the edifying philosopher towards someone who thinks that science is rational and that edification is not. In such a case, where there is no common ground between the opponents, all that edifying philosophers can do is 'to show how the other side looks from our point of view. That is, all we can do is be hermeneutic about the opposition – trying to show how the odd or paradoxical or offensive things they say hang together with the rest of what they want to say, and how what they say looks when put in our own alternative idiom. This sort of hermeneutics with polemical intent is common to Heidegger's and Derrida's attempts to deconstruct the tradition'.

It is noteworthy that Rorty speaks of 'how the other side looks', and of putting what they say 'in our own alternative idiom'; there is no question of failing to understanding what they mean. One can now see how important it is for Rorty that 'commensurable' shall *not* be defined in terms of sameness of meaning.[56] Edifying philosophers understand the meaning of their opponents' terms, yet their discourses are not commensurable. However, this is by the way. Let us suppose that Rorty does understand the things said by the other side; what does he do about them? It seems to me that, however hard Rorty tries to bury the old Adam – I mean, the tendency to *argue* with those who disagree with one – he does not succeed. According to Rorty, the edifying philosopher shows how the 'odd or paradoxical' things that his opponents say 'hang together' with other things that they say. But what would be the point of this? Does Rorty think that his opponents can't see how their own views hang together? It seems to me that Rorty's views make sense only if we take him to be saying to his opponent, 'Your views, when their logical consequences are worked out, lead to self-contradiction'. This interpretation is strengthened by the reference to Derrida and his attempts at 'deconstruction'. Talking of Derrida's analysis of Husserl's theory of signs, Jonathan Culler writes, 'Derrida's analysis is what we now call a "deconstruction" of Husserl's text; a demonstration that the logic of Husserl's argument "undoes" itself and thus involves a central paradox or self-contradiction which is a basic insight into the matter under discussion'.[57] In sum, it seems that Rorty is here inclining towards the view that his opponent's discourse is self-contradictory, and as such should be rejected as false. In other words, Rorty is assuming that there are some principles that are common to rational discourse, and the 'conversation' of which he speaks turns out to be Socratic after all.

But this, as I have said, is not Rorty's official view of what conversation in philosophy is like. If we want to understand that view, we shall find it helpful to look at Rorty's account of the way in which the history of philosophy should be written. This account is of particular interest in that it has wider implications for humanistic education in general. Rorty is of course opposed to the idea[58] that historians of philosophy should sit in judgement on previous philosophers; he is also opposed to that view of the history of philosophy which sees it as a series of attempted solutions to problems. Edifying philosophy, he says, will deal in 'books, not problems'.[59] Rorty wants to present philosophers, not as people who argue, but as people who have 'world-views'. This is how he can talk of such 'edifying philosophers' as Marx, Freud and Sartre,[60] and it explains how Nietzsche and Kierkegaard can figure among the philosophers of whom Rorty approves.[61]

What is one to make of all this? The queston is a big one, and I must be brief. Briefly, then, I think that Rorty is right in emphasising that philosophers do have views, if not of the world as a whole, at any rate of man, and that these views are of abiding interest. To come back to the question posed by the student of the history of philosophy which was mentioned earlier: we go to philosophers, not just for their arguments, but for their world-views. But the issue is not one that concerns philosophy alone. World-views are not the exclusive prerogative of philosophers; they are embodied in the works of (for example) poets, novelists, artists, historians and critics – in sum, in everything that is the stuff of humanistic education. This part of Rorty's book is, I believe, of real value; but it suffers from being embedded in a relativist framework which is not self-consistent, and which Rorty himself finds troublesome.

NOTES

1. Richard Rorty, *Philosophy and the Mirror of Nature* (Princeton and Oxford, 1980).
2. Ibid., p. 362.
3. Ibid., cf. p. 359n.
4. Ibid., p. 173.
5. Ibid., pp. 168n., 173.
6. Ibid., p. 11.
7. Ibid., p. 370.
8. Ibid., p. 372.
9. Ibid., p. 315.
10. See, e.g., Kant, *Critique of Pure Reason*, A106.
11. Rorty, op. cit., p. 315.
12. Ibid., p. 272.
13. Ibid., p. 381.
14. Ibid., pp. 9–10.
15. Ibid., p. 269.
16. Kuhn, *The Structure of Scientific Revolutions*, 2nd edn (Chicago, 1970).
17. Rorty, op. cit., p. 316.
18. Ibid., p. 316n.
19. Hilary Putnam, *Reason, Truth and History* (Cambridge 1981) pp. 114ff.
20. Rorty, op. cit., p. 317.
21. Ibid., pp. 328 ff.
22. Ibid., cf. p. 329.
23. Ibid., p. 329.
24. Ibid., p. 331.
25. Ibid., p. 330.
26. Ibid., 330–1.
27. Ibid., p. 332.
28. Ibid., cf. p. 288.
29. W. V. Quine, 'On Empirically Equivalent Systems of the World', *Erkenntnis*, 9, pp. 327–8. Quoted by W. H. Newton-Smith, *The Rationality of Science* (London, 1981) p. 181.
30. Rorty, op. cit., p. 357.
31. Gadamer, *Truth and Method* (New York, 1975) p. xi; Rorty, op. cit., p. 358.
32. Rorty, op. cit., p. 357.
33. Ibid., p. 358.
34. Ibid., p. 358.
35. Ibid., p. 359.
36. Ibid., p. 361.
37. Ibid., p. 361.
38. Ibid., cf. p. 363.
39. Ibid., p. 269.
40. Ibid., p. 356.
41. Cf. ibid., p. 382 on 'normal science'.
42. Ibid., p. 360.
43. Ibid., pp. 370–1.

44. Ibid., p. 370.
45. Ibid., p. 173.
46. Ibid., p. 370.
47. Ibid., p. 371.
48. Ibid., p. 359n.
49. Ibid., pp. 362–3.
50. See, e.g. P. B. Medawar, 'Hypothesis and Imagination', in *the Art of the Soluble* (Penguin Books, 1969); Reprinted in Medawar, *Pluto's Republic* (Oxford, 1982).
51. Rorty, op. cit., cf. p. 358.
52. Ibid., cf. p. 364.
53. Ibid., p. 347.
54. Ibid., p. 170. Cf. ibid., p. 315.
55. Ibid., pp. 364–5.
56. Ibid., p. 316n, quoted above.
57. J. Sturrock (ed.), *Structuralism and Since* (Oxford, 1979) p. 159.
58. Rorty, op. cit., p. 391.
59. Ibid., p. 394.
60. Ibid., p. 386.
61. Ibid., p. 369.

Part III
Reason in Religious and Moral Education

7 Two Questions about Religious Education

W. D. HUDSON

The questions I want to discuss are whether or not religious education *can*, and *should*, be part of what goes on in schools. These questions are important in themselves and the answers which I personally would give to them will become apparent as we proceed; but they are also important because they bring into focus more general questions, such as how we are to conceive of education as a whole and how we are to select, from among all the subjects which could conceivably be part of the school curriculum, those which we think ought to be. It is arguable that these larger questions are always best approached, not in the abstract, but with specific issues in mind like that which I have raised in my opening sentence. Such, at all events, is the way in which I intend to approach them here.

Equally intelligent and well-informed contemporary philosophers of education are divided in their attitudes to religious education. Some – Paul Hirst[1] for example – take the view that religion is not a form of knowledge and so has no place in the curriculum, at any rate of schools that are maintained by the state; whereas others – Mary Warnock[2] for example – are disposed to think that the time is ripe for a renaissance of religious education because it could bring a breath of inspiration into the dull and unimaginative lives which so many of the children in our schools lead. As I indicated at the beginning, I think there are two issues which have to be faced in making up one's mind which of these conflicting opinions one agrees with. When I asked just now whether religious education *can* be part of what goes on in schools, I meant this 'can' to be a logical one. The question I intended to raise was whether the idea of religious education is logically compatible with our concept of education in general. And when I went on to ask whether it not only can, but also *should*, be part of

what goes on in schools, I meant this 'should' to be evaluational.
What I wanted to put at issue was whether, out of all the subjects
which could conceivably be taught in schools, we are justified – by
our normal criteria of selection – in giving religion a place in the
curriculum. I will take up these two questions in turn.

I

Before doing so, however, I ought to say more precisely what I take
'religious education' to mean – once it is delivered from certain
confusions which becloud it – and why. In order to do this I need to
draw two distinctions. Firstly, the distinction between what I would
call respectively 'education *about* religion' and 'education *in* religion'.
By education *about* religion I mean, for example, telling one's pupils
that such-and-such beliefs about the supernatural have been held by
such-and-such people at such-and-such a time and that these beliefs
have had such-and-such an effect on the course of their history, the
content of their literature and art, the political conflicts or social
upheavals in which they have become embroiled, and so on. By
education *in* religion, on the other hand, I mean teaching one's pupils
how to differentiate religious questions and answers from those of
other kinds, how to think for oneself in religious terms, and how
thereby to put oneself in the way of the sort of experience, or the kind
of value judgments, which such thinking can generate. I realise, of
course, that the distinction I have drawn here between 'about' and
'in' may not be as hard and fast as I have made it appear; in telling his
pupils about the effects religion has had on other people a teacher
may well be giving them some awareness of what it is like to think
religiously for oneself and, in explaining the latter, he may well find
himself telling them something about the influence religion has had
on other people. Nevertheless the distinction is a real one.

It seems clear to me that it is appropriate to take the expression
'religious education' to mean education *in* religion rather than merely
education *about* it. Indeed, I regard it as a misnomer to call the latter
religious education at all because, even though its subject-matter may
be religious belief, its treatment of that subject-matter is more
accurately described as historical, literary, political (or whatever)
education than as religious. To take a parallel case, suppose a teacher
gave his class lessons on the effects which scientific inventions – say,
from that of the wheel to that of the nuclear bomb – have had on

human life. He could conceivably do this without giving them even the most elementary instruction in how to think scientifically for themselves. But, in such case, would anyone describe what he had given them as scientific education? Similarly, I think that only education *in* religion, as I have defined it above, can properly be called religious education.

The second distinction I need to draw is between what I will call respectively 'becoming educated in religion' and 'becoming religious (or a religious believer)'. When I speak of someone 'becoming educated *in* religion' – as I explained just now – I mean that he is learning how to think for himself in religious terms. But I must add that I do not mean that he will necessarily go on to do so with any degree of conviction or commitment. Just as it is possible for somebody who has had a scientific education not to think scientifically about the practical problems that arise in his own life; and just as it is possible for people, like Henry Ford, who know how to look at things in a historical perspective, nevertheless to feel that 'history is bunk'; so it is possible for someone, who has been taught how to think for himself in religious terms, to choose not to do so. By contrast, when I speak of somebody 'becoming religious' I mean that he is not only learning how to think for himself in religious terms but coming to do so as a committed religious believer.

The job of a religious educator is that of enabling his pupils to 'become educated in religion' rather than that of persuading them to 'become religious'. There are those – preachers and evangelists – who quite properly pursue this latter aim. All I wish to point out is that there is a logical distinction between what they are doing and what a religious educator exists to do. No doubt, what preachers and evangelists do logically presupposes what religious educators exist to do, since there is no point in trying to persuade people to become religious unless they have been given some idea of how to do so; and again, in practice, preachers and evangelists doubtless sometimes function as religious educators no less than as advocates of religious belief; but the fact remains that there is a clear distinction between teaching people how to think or act for themselves in a certain way and persuading them actually to do so. It seems clear that it is appropriate to take the expression 'religious education' to mean an activity of the former, rather than of the latter, kind.

For these reasons, then, I think we are entitled to tighten up the meaning of the expression 'religious education' so that it signifies the process which I have described as that of becoming educated *in* religion, as distinct, on the one hand, from merely becoming furnished with information *about* it, and, on the other, from becoming a convinced or committed religious believer. In considering the opinions I shall voice in the remainder of this chapter, it is most important to bear in mind that it is religious education in this sense of which I am speaking and not in some other.

II

I come now to the former of the two questions raised in my opening sentence: *can* religious education, as I have just defined it, be part of what goes on in schools? That is to say, is it logically compatible with our concept of education in general?

The word 'education' has a virtually constant evaluative meaning (whatever is so described is thereby normally commended) and a variable descriptive meaning (many different activities have in their time been called by this name). In consequence, the word admits, not only of stipulative, but also of persuasive, definition. Writers on education frequently fasten on certain activities or states of affairs, of which they happen to approve, and contend that these are what 'education' really means, or at least that they are the goods which a 'true' or 'real' education would deliver. However, when used in the way that interests us here – that is, as the name for what goes on in schools – the word 'education' has a fairly stable meaning. It is invariably conceived to be a process of initiation; and, if we ask, 'Initiation into what?', the answers given, though varied, are always systematic forms of reasoning or behaviour – that is, subjects like history or science and activities like games or craft. Sometimes 'education' is comprehensively defined as initiation into forms of knowledge.[3] There is perhaps no great harm in this definition, provided we bear in mind that knowledge can be either knowledge-*how* or knowledge-*that*.[4] But if education is thought of simply as initiation into various forms of knowledge-*that*, then this in my opinion is a great mistake. To remove the possibility of its being made, I prefer to drop the word 'knowledge' altogether and to define education as 'initiation into various kinds of understanding'. In attempting to say what I mean by this I shall now present certain thoughts which reveal the influence of Wittgenstein's later philosophical writings.[5]

Wittgenstein imagines[6] the following simple example of what we would quite naturally describe as a moment of understanding. One person, A (we will suppose him to be a schoolmaster) writes down the following sequence of numbers: 1, 5, 11, 19, 29. Another person, B (we will suppose him to be a boy in A's class) exclaims at this point, 'Now I can go on!.' The question Wittenstein raises is what we would mean by describing this as a moment of understanding.

Some may reply that we would mean that B says 'Now I can go on!' because he understands.[7] If that is so, they can be called upon to give some account of the nature of this cause, described as 'he understands'. A number of physical and mental events, which could conceivably occur in conjunction with B's remark 'Now I can go on!', may suggest themselves as possible accounts. For example, just before B makes that remark, the formation rule of A's series of numbers, namely, $a_n = n^2 + n - 1$, may have occurred to him. Is that then what 'he understands' means? Again, as B is saying 'Now I can go on!', a feeling of tension, which has been building up as he watches A writing down his series of numbers, may suddenly find release. So, is that what 'he understands' means? Yet again, just after B says 'Now I can go on!', he may say, 'The next number in the series is 41.' But can any of these supposed events – or other similar ones which we might imagine – be correctly taken for the cause referred to by 'he understands'? Clearly not. The expression 'he understands' is not equivalent in meaning to any or all of them because it would make perfectly good sense for someone to say that B had understood, even though none of them had occurred; or alternatively, to say that B had not understood, even though all of them had occurred. Therefore, what 'he understands' refers to must be something other or more than they.[8] But what more or other? All we seem to be left with is B's claim to be able to go on. Does that constitute his understanding? It may seem that Wittgenstein thought so for he appears to regard 'Now I can go on' and 'Now I understand' as synonymous.[9] But the matter is rather more complicated than that and we must go into it a little more deeply.

In order to do so it is necessary to digress for a moment and to say something about Wittgenstein's conception of 'criteria'. Throughout his later writings he worked with the idea that the meaning of a sign (i.e. a sentence) is to be looked for in what he called its criteria and not, as he had supposed in his earlier writings, in its truth-, or verification-, conditions. What precisely he meant by criteria is a matter of some dispute but it may be safely said that his basic idea was as follows. The meaning of a sign is to be located through its inter-connexions with other signs in the system of signs to which it belongs. Very broadly speaking, the criteria for any given sentence may be of three alternative kinds;[10] namely, (i) sentences which it would generally be thought appropriate to use in conjunction with the given sign; (ii) those which it would generally be thought appropriate to use in response to it; and (iii) ones which describe circumstances in which it would be generally considered appropriate for the given sign to find utterance. To take the simplest possible kind of example. If the remark 'My feet ache' were the given sign, then 'I want to bathe them' would illustrate the first kind of criterion; 'Put them in hot water', the second; and 'He (i.e. the speaker of the given sign) has walked a long way', the third. The meaning of a sentence is thus determined by other sentences, belonging to the same system of sentences, which are, or could be, articulated in the same context. This is what people mean when they say that the later Wittgenstein thought of meaning is intra-linguistic. To use his own metaphor, it is only as part of a system of signs that a sign has *life*.[11]

Returning now to my claim that education should be defined as 'initiation into various kinds of understanding', it is clear that, if we accept Wittgenstein's criterial account of meaning, we must – in order to appreciate the force of this definition – consider what would generally be regarded as the appropriate criteria for such sentences as 'He understands' or 'I understand.' To take 'He understands' first, let us suppose that someone says of B 'He understands how to continue A's series of numbers.' This is a description. Putting things very simply, it could be taken for an inference, if the criterial sentence 'B has successfully continued many series of the same kind already' could also be said in the same context; or, alternatively, for a prediction, if 'B will be able to continue A's series' could. These two examples of criterial sentences are instances of the third kind noted above: that is to say, they describe the circumstances – what B has done or will do – in which the given sentence is being said and thereby determine its meaning as either an inference or a prediction.

But now take 'I understand' and suppose B himself says 'I understand how to continue A's series.' This too could conceivably be a descriptive inference or prediction. But the point I wish to make is that it need not be; and, in a typical classroom situation, it will not be. Note, in passing, that this sentence is equivalent in meaning to 'Now I can go on!', as used by Wittgenstein in the above example. When I say that it need not, and in a typical classroom situation will not, be an inference or a prediction, what I have in mind is this. It could conceivably be said by B on the *first* occasion that he is confronted by a series of the kind A writes down. And, in that case, it could not possibly be an inference from B's past success in continuing series of the same kind. Will it therefore be meaningless? Surely not! Then again, suppose, having uttered this sentence, B *gets things wrong* – e.g. by giving 42 instead of 41 as the next number in the series. In that case, if his remark were a prediction, it would be a false one and to that extent an inappropriate thing for him to have said. But is it always inappropriate for a schoolboy to say 'I understand', if he subsequently gets things wrong? If we say it is, we are in effect saying that he should never claim to be able to answer a question in class unless he not only *thinks* he knows the right answer, but *really does* so. And surely that is absurd! Considerations of a somewhat similar kind to these led Wittgenstein to say, in effect, that 'I understand', when uttered in what I have called a typical classroom situation, is not descriptive at all, by way of either inference or prediction, but is in fact what he called an 'avowal' or a 'signal'.[12] To grasp what he means, it may be helpful to note that B's sentence 'I understand how to continue A's series' means much the same as it would have meant if B, instead of saying anything, had simply put up his hand in class.

According to Wittgenstein's criterial account of meaning, the sentence 'I understand', taken for a signal, only has meaning, like any other sentence, in so far as it has criteria. And if we wish to grasp its meaning, we must ask, as Wittgenstein puts it: 'in what sort of case, in what kind of circumstances, do we say 'Now I know how to go on' ... ?'[13] The two following very simple examples may show us in which direction to look for answers to this question. Suppose a schoolmaster and one of his pupils have been walking along a street in silence for some time and the pupil suddenly exclaims, 'Now I understand!' The schoolmaster is surprised. 'What do you mean?' he asks. The schoolboy explains that he has been thinking about a question he could not answer in class but which now he thinks he can. This explanation gives his remark meaning. But if he could give no such explanation it would be pointless. Now, secondly, suppose a second-form pupil, known to be of only average ability, is for some reason sitting at the back of the room in which a physics class for the upper sixth is in progress. The master taking the class writes a complicated formula on the board and asks the sixth-formers to explain it. 'I understand!' pipes up the second-former. Heads are turned and eyebrows raised. What does he mean, he understands?

How can he possibly understand until he has studied physics for four more years? What I am endeavouring to bring out by these two simple examples is that, in a classroom situation, the signal 'I understand' has meaning where two circumstances obtain. One is that some systematic form of reasoning or behaviour is in progress (this was fulfilled in the former example in so far as the schoolboy was still thinking about what had been going on in the classroom). The other, that the person who says 'I understand' has already had explained to him enough about the relevant form of reasoning or behaviour for it to be realistic to expect him to grasp what is going on at the moment (this was not fulfilled in the latter example in so far as the schoolboy was merely an average second-former). A schoolboy's 'I understand how to go on' has meaning only within a system of signs which includes some such criterial sentences as 'He is a member of a science (or whatever) class' and 'He is up to the standard of what is going on there at the moment.' Given the fulfilment of these criterial conditions the meaning of the schoolboy's remark is clear. It is a signal indicating his will to participate in what is going on. Even if he has never successfully participated in this kind of thing in the past and even if, when called upon to do so now, he gets things wrong, his signal will have meaning as an indication of his will to participate.

What I have just been saying about 'I understand', taken for a signal, brings into focus two important points about understanding, namely its connexion with intelligence and with rationality. To take the former, it shows how understanding is contingent upon intelligence. A teacher cannot give his pupils understanding; he can only try to bring it within their reach. If we understand anything, we must do so for ourselves; no one else can do it for us. After a teacher has done all he can to make it meaningful for his pupils to signal 'I understand', some of them will still deliver the signal oftener than others; and of those who deliver it, some will in the event go on successfully oftener than others. It may be that a teacher should divide his time and attention equally among his pupils, irrespective of their varying ability; but what he cannot do is initiate them into equal shares of understanding all round, for understanding depends on intelligence and intelligence varies.

Then again, the interpretation of 'I understand' as a signal brings out the fact that understanding is essentially self-critical, just as rationality is. When anyone, in a classroom situation, signals 'I understand', he thereby puts himself on trial. In so far as this signal is synonymous with 'Now I can go on!', the claim implicit within it may or may not be fulfilled in the event. The one who has given the signal may find that he lacks the ability to go on successfully. But not only that. It may be that the defect is not in him but in the systematic form of reasoning or behaviour into which he has been hitherto initiated. Sometimes such a system proves inadequate to the questions or problems which arise within it and, in consequence, needs to be revised. I have argued elsewhere[14] that learning to be rational means learning at one and the same time to conform to a system of theoretical or practical rules and to subject this system to critical testing. When anyone signals 'I understand', he is putting such learning into effect; for he is undertaking to think in accordance with some system and thereby to test, not only his own ability to apply it, but also the adequacy of the system to the kind of question or problem with which he has hitherto been taught that it can deal.

This discussion of 'I understand', as a signal, has been necessary in order to make clear what I mean when I offer 'initiation into various kinds of understanding' as the most appropriate definition of what goes on in schools. To initiate a pupil into understanding is, in my submission, to provide the criterial conditions which make it meaningful for him to signal 'I understand'. These criterial conditions in all their complexity will differ from subject to subject, of course, but they will always include ones of the two kinds I have mentioned above. It is a school teacher's job, whatever his subject, firstly to create for his pupils a situation in which some systematic form of reasoning or behaviour is in progress; and secondly, to ensure that enough has been explained to them about what is going on for it to be realistic to expect them to be able to participate. Teachers exist to provide contexts in which their pupils can exercise their own intelligence and rationality by participating of their own volition in some systematic form of reasoning or behaviour.

If that is how we conceive of education in general, it seems clear that the answer to the former of our two main questions is in the affirmative: religious education *can* be part of what goes on in schools. The word 'religion' is sometimes used disparagingly nowadays in places where one might have least expected it to be so; some christian evangelists, for example, contrast it unfavourably with 'faith' and some christian educationalists, with 'spirituality'. But such talk is, for the most part, hopelessly muddled. The concept of religion is perfectly clear in its normal meaning. Any instantiation of it purports to answer two kinds of question, namely 'Why are things so?' and 'How ought we to act.' It answers those of the former kind with indicative explanations deduced from its basic presuppositions concerning existence; and those of the latter kind, with imperative judgments drawn from its first principles concerning conduct. A religion is, therefore, a systematic form of reasoning and behaviour. Initiation into an understanding of it, as such, is, in principle, the same sort of process as initiation into any other kind of understanding. Teachers of religion exist, like those of other subjects, to provide the criterial conditions in which their pupils can meaningfully deliver the signal "I understand". This is a job which can be done, though not perhaps an easy one.

III

I come then to the second of our two main questions: namely, *should* religious education be part of what goes on in schools? So far, all I have shown is that it *can* be. However, there are many other subjects which could conceivably have a place in the school curriculum but in fact do not. So, what reason, if any, is there why religious education should? In my earlier comments on this question, I spoke of 'our normal criteria of selection' and that remark may have suggested that I think of these criteria as precisely defined and rigorously applied. But, of course, I know they are not. The general question of what criterion (or criteria) should be applied in selecting subjects for inclusion in the school curriculum seems nowadays to be as divisive as the particular question of whether or not religious education should be included. So we really have two questions on our hands not just one: namely, what should the general criterion (or criteria) be? and, does religious education fulfil it (or them)? I want to suggest three conceivable answers to the more general question and to apply them to the particular case of religious education in turn.

(i) The first conceivable answer, expressed as succinctly as possible, is that the general criterion should be *what society wants*. Education, whatever else it may, or may not, be, is indisputably a form of socialisation. As such, it will necessarily share the twin objectives at which any society under normal conditions aims, namely self-preservation and adaptation. A society seeks both to perpetuate its own identity and to accommodate itself to the changing conditions of the world in which it exists. What it wants from education, therefore, will be the initiation of its young into a balance between kinds of understanding which fulfil the former objective and kinds which fulfil the latter. On the one hand, for example, it will want them to have an understanding of the language, literature, history, customs, etc., which give it its distinctive and continuing identity; and on the other, of such sciences or techniques as will enable those of its members who understand them to survive and prosper in their generation. A discussion document, recently (September, 1984) issued by the Department of Education, entitled *The Organisation and Content of the 5–16 Curriculum*, exemplifies what I have in mind. This document manifestly aims at both the continuation of certain subjects which have traditionally been part of our school curriculum and the introduction of new ones – or the giving of new prominence to certain existing ones – that are considered important for the future well-being of our society. Among the proposals it puts forward are the following: English and Mathematics to be compulsory for all children throughout their schooldays; all pupils to be introduced to the three sciences of Biology, Chemistry and Physics and none to give up science whilst still at school; Computer Studies to be recognised as essential; opportunities to study Craft, Design and Technology to be available throughout the school. By contrast, however, only some pupils to study a foreign language; History and Geography to take a secondary place; Music, Art and Drama not necessarily to be available throughout the whole school. The document puts these and other proposals forward for discussion, not exclusively to self-styled authorities, but to our society as a whole. The view that this is the right thing to do – that the general criterion is what society wants – has this much to be said for it at the very least: it avoids the error of supposing that there are certain objective facts from which the proper content of the curriculum can be deduced. I am thinking of such erroneous opinions as that human nature can be analysed into elements – reason, will, emotion, or whatever – and that the curriculum must therefore include subjects which will enlighten and direct each of these in turn; or the opinion that knowledge can be divided into a limited number of specific forms, each of which must therefore be accommodated in the timetable. There are, of course, some objective facts that are relevant to what goes on in schools; but they are about what can (as distinct from what ought to) do so. They are facts about child psychology, for example, which determine how much can be learned and under what conditions. These facts, in so far as they can be reliably discovered, will affect a well-informed teacher's methods; and they will restrict the aims which any sensible person thinks education should pursue since there is no point in aiming at that which cannot be achieved. But they will not tell us which, out of all the various kinds of understanding, are the ones into which children should be initiated at school. That is a value judgment, not a deduction from matters of fact. And I think there is a good deal to be said for the view that it is one which any society as a whole must make for its young.

The discussion document, to which I referred just now, listed Religious Education, along with English and Mathematics, as a compulsory subject for all pupils throughout their schooldays. Since less than ten per cent of our population attend a place of worship with any regularity it might be thought that this proposal will be rejected. But all the evidence is to the contrary. The overwhelming majority of our people, when consulted, have hitherto been firmly in favour of religious education in schools and there is little or no reason to suppose that they have changed their minds. Some commentators on public opinion see this as a classic example of its irrationality or hypocrisy. How can those to whom religion manifestly counts for so little themselves sincerely want their children to be educated in it? But for my part I see this as neither irrational nor hypocritical. Even though a subject has become of little or no significance to a man himself, it does not necessarily argue any lack of reason or sincerity on his part, if he wishes his children to be taught their way about in it. There are, after all, many subjects which we were taught at school but in which many of us have now lost interest; but we do not therefore demand that they should be removed from the school curriculum. And so, even if all we ourselves can hear is the 'melancholy, long, withdrawing roar' of the sea of faith, we may, without either irrationality or hypocrisy, want our children to be given some understanding of that sea's ancient charts in case, for them, the tide should once again flow at the full. The day may come, of course, when it seems absurd to our society as a whole to allow of that possibility any longer. But it has not come yet. And if religious education in schools is what our society wants, is there any more authoritative criterion by appeal to which we are entitled to say that it should not be part of what goes on there?

(ii) Some may say that a more authoritative general criterion is *what appeals to the interests and inclinations of the pupils themselves*. For some time now there has been a vociferous lobby in favour of child-centred education. Many are the gradations of opinion within it but the basic idea is that what goes on in schools should satisfy the inherent interests and inclinations of the pupils, rather than impose upon them the value judgments of their society. Wittgenstein's teaching methods, for example, when he worked as a village schoolmaster from 1920 to 1926, were influenced by such opinions and, in particular, by the two main principles of the Austrian School Reform Movement, namely, 'self-activity' and 'integrated instruction'.[15] According to the former, a teacher ought to encourage his pupis to think things out for themselves rather than drill them in their studies; and according to the latter, he should be free to go from one subject to another, as questions arise in the course of the day, rather than be bound by a timetable. Such ideas have been widely canvassed for more than half a century and they have, beyond doubt, had some beneficial consequences.

However, the idea that this is a better general criterion than what society wants must, to say the least, be approached with some caution. There is something to be said for it, of course. Firm evidence exists that, so far as teaching methods are concerned, some of these appeal to the interests and inclinations of pupils in general more effectively than others do and consequently result in more rapid or retentive learning. Then again, there is evidence that, so far as the content of their education is concerned, children differ to some extent in their individual interests and inclinations and, if they are allowed, especially in the later stages of their school career, to specialise in subjects of their own choice within the curriculum, most of them will study more successfully than they otherwise would. But it certainly does not follow from such considerations that the content of any child's curriculum should be determined solely by his own interests or inclinations. Apart from the practical difficulties of any such arrangement, there is good reason to think that the children in later life might regret that they had ever been subjected to it. One's interests and inclinations, especially in early life, are often ephemeral and ill-informed. We all need the wisdom and experience of our society to guide us in what it is desirable that we should learn.

Those responsible for religious education sometimes complain that their hardest task is arousing and retaining in their pupils an interest in their subject and an inclination to study it seriously. The reasons they give for this state of affairs range from the prevailing materialism of our time to the scant regard that is paid to O and A levels in religious studies by employers and admissions tutors. I suppose these are facts of life which, for the present at any rate, have to be accepted. All I would say about them here is that they do not constitute a proof that religious education is inherently uninteresting.

By 'inherently' I mean, as the kind of intellectual discipline which it is appropriate to have in the school curriculum. Most other school subjects are regarded as uninteresting or valueless by some pupils but this is not considered a good reason for discontinuing them. What I am saying is that there is no good reason to regard religious education as necessarily more boring or useless than any other subject.

Two points about it need to be made, or so it seems to me. One, that, within the framework of the presuppositions of a religion such as Christianity, the quest for acceptable explanations of what goes on in the world, or for enlightened applications of certain definitive principles of conduct, can be as subtle and fascinating an intellectual exercise as the quest, say, for scientific explanations of natural phenomena, or for historical accounts of what went on in the past. The other point is that, if attention were centred in the classroom on working out what such explanations or applications must be, instead of on often ill-informed, second-order discussions about whether or not God exists, this might well add to the interest of the subject. It really is rather curious, when one thinks about it, that religious education, unlike any other school subject, seems to be obsessed with second-order issues that belong to philosophy rather than religion. Contrast it in this respect with history, for example. Historical explanations presuppose intentional action and free agency: they are about what certain people did and why. But no one thinks that history lessons, even in the upper forms, should be taken up with discussions about whether or not there is any such thing as free agency or intentional action. This is a complicated and contentious philosophical question. The history master simply lays it aside and gets on with teaching history – and quite rightly. What I am suggesting is that teachers of religious education should get on with teaching their subject too and not be diverted into necessarily half-baked philosophical discussions about its presuppositions. The time will come for school children to philosophise about religion when they know what it is.

(iii) For want of a better name, I shall call the third conception of the general criterion that of *conformity to certain normative concepts*. Unlike the two conceptions of it to which I have just referred, this third one does not turn simply on a matter of empirical fact – 'Does society want this subject in the curriculum' or 'Does it appeal to the interests and inclinations of the pupils?' – but on the analysis of certain normative concepts. It tests any candidate for inclusion by whether or not its inclusion would be logically compatible with what is meant by one, or more, of these concepts. The concepts themselves are taken to be implied by the very concept of education; and conformity to them is therefore deemed to be a logical necessity on the ground that it would be self-contradictory to say that any norm which is implied by the concept of education itself should not determine the school curriculum. Those who propose this third version of the general criterion recognise that it may cut across what society wants, or what interests the pupils, but they are not deterred by that. To their way of thinking, what is meant by 'education' overrides all other considerations, when it comes to what should go on in schools. They contend that the concepts they take to be normative need to be clearly analysed and then applied as norms in deciding upon the proper content of the curriculum. Let me now be more specific and briefly refer to three such putatively normative concepts in turn.

The first is the concept of what it is to be a human being. This concept is implicit in the widely held view that education means learning to be a human being (or a person); for we cannot explain this definition without saying what we mean by being a human being. Any analysis of this latter concept will necessarily include some account of the systematic forms of reasoning or behaviour in which we consider it definitive of a human being to engage. These forms will all be instances of what I called earlier 'kinds of understanding' and, if education is described as learning to be a human being, initiation into them will therefore be part, if not the whole, of what that description means. The general criterion, then, of whether or not any subject should be part of what goes on in schools will become whether or not it is one such subject. And the particular question of whether or not education *in* religion should go on in schools will become whether or not some understanding of how to think or act in a religious way is as essential to our conception of an educated human being as some understanding of, say, how to reason scientifically or to judge morally.

A second normative concept is that of what it is for a discipline to be rational. This concept is implicit in the widely held view that education means learning to be rational; for we cannot explain this definition without saying what we take a rational discipline to be. The analysis of rationality is a complicated undertaking but if initiation into a theoretical discipline such as scientific inquiry, or into a practical one such as playing a game like soccer, are acceptable as paradigm cases of learning to be rational, then it is fairly easy to indicate some of the common features which make them so. For one, every such discipline is based on certain stateable presuppositions which do not contradict one another (e.g. the constitutive concepts and rules of inference of physical science; or the definitions of victory and defeat and the rules of procedure, which make a game like soccer what it is). Another common feature of rational disciplines is that they require consistent adherence to their presuppositions. And a third is that they admit of some revision of these presuppositions, where adherence to them appears to be defeating its own purpose (e.g. where the accepted presuppositions of some form of scientific inquiry seem inadequate to the natural phenomena they are invoked to explain; or the existing rules of a game like soccer are being appealed to in ways which take the pleasure or excitement out of it). Once analysis has made some such common features of a rational discipline, *qua* rational, plain to us, we can make the question whether any given subject possesses them our general criterion for inclusion in the school curriculum. And, if that is the general criterion, then the particular question about religious education becomes whether or not religion can be regarded as a systematic form of reasoning or behaviour possessed of these common features also. That is to say, whether or not it too is logically grounded in certain non-contradictory presuppositions, to which consistent adherence is ordinarily required, but which, if they prove inadequate to experience, are open to some degree of revision.

A third normative concept is that of the curriculum itself, conceived as a unified whole. This concept is implied by the widely held view that education is – or ought to be – of the whole child; for we cannot explain that definition without giving some indication of how the elements of a curriculum can be unified in order to achieve it. The unification of the curriculum may, of course, be conceived simply to consist in the fact that its constituent subjects complement one another by providing, one by one, for the education of the several, separate aspects of the whole child. But I think this unification can – and should – be seen as a more dynamic inter-relationship than that. To borrow a metaphor, which Wittgenstein[16] uses in a different, though not entirley unrelated, connexion, the subjects in the curriculum can be seen as 'a riverbed of thoughts', the component parts of which direct cross-currents upon one another. The notion of 'integrated instruction' to which I referred a few moments ago – i.e. of one subject leading to another – exemplifies what I mean by the possibility of a more dynamic interrelationship, as does the notion

that inter-disciplinary university courses can result in a more profound understanding of the disciplines combined.

If the subjects in a curriculum are to form a unified whole, they
must at the very least not contradict one another in their content. To
take the very simplest sort of example, if religion explains the
existence of the physical world as due to God's creation, then what it
says about how He created it must not contradict what is said about
the nature of that world in sciences such as biology, chemistry, etc.
Where, if anywhere, two subjects appear to contradict one another in
their content, adjustments must be made on one side or the other – or
possibly on both. The general criterion for inclusion in the curriculum
therefore becomes how responsive a subject is able to be to such
cross-currents. Of course, this is a very complicated matter and there
is more, much more, to be said about it but this much can be said
about it here: if a subject purports to override the whole of mankind's
intellectual endeavour and to have the right to subordinate the
content of every other subject to its own presuppositions, then – by
the present normative concept – it should not be part of what goes on
in schools. The particular question about religious education is
whether or not religion is, inherently and necessarily, such a subject.

IV

In conclusion, may I say that I think these various formulations of the
general criterion can all be regarded as necessary conditions for
admission to the curriculum; and that, if all are met, they add up to as
near a sufficient condition as we may get. A subject, that is to say,
should not be part of what goes on in schools unless: (i) its inclusion is
what the majority of people in the relevant society want; (ii) the
subject itself is not inherently less appealing to the interests and
inclinations of the pupils than most other subjects; (iii) it accords with
the normative concepts of what it is to be a human being, a rational
discipline, and a unified curriculum.

Does religious education fulfil these necessary conditions? My own
opinion is that it does. But I do not offer that opinion glibly; I know
that it takes some defending, especially where the normative concepts, referred to just now, come into play. Elsewhere, in various
contexts,[17] I have tried to defend the thesis that religion – conceived
as a systematic form of reasoning and behaviour – is not fatally
dissimilar in its logical structure to other disciplines which, no one

would deny, are equal partners in mankind's intellectual endeavour. Whatever may be thought of these efforts of mine, the point I wish to make here is that this is the frontier which those who advocate religious education must come out into the open and try to defend, rather than retreat into the thickets of vague talk about spirituality, or whatever.

NOTES

1. See P. H. Hirst, *Knowledge and the Curriculum* (London, 1974) p. 181.
2. See Mary Warnock, *Education: a Way Ahead* (Oxford, 1979) p. 77.
3. Hirst, op. cit., *passim*.
4. See Gilbert Ryle, *The Concept of Mind* (London, 1949) ch. II.
5. See especially *Philosophical Investigations*, i, 143 ff.
6. Op. cit., i. 151.
7. Op. cit., i. 153.
8. Op. cit., i. 152b.
9. Op. cit., i. 154a.
10. Cf. G. P. Baker and P. M. S. Hacker, Wittgenstein: *Meaning and Understanding* (Oxford, 1983) ch. II.
11. *The Blue Book* (Oxford, 1960) p. 5.
12. *Investigations*, i, 180–1.
13. Op. cit., i. 154c.
14. Cf. my 'Learning to be Rational', *Proceedings of the Philosophy of Education Society of Great Britain*, vol. xi, 1977.
15. For an account of Wittgenstein's activities as a schoolmaster, see W. W. Bartley III, *Wittgenstein* (New York, 1973) ch. 3; and his 'Theory of Language and Philosophy of Science as Instruments of Educational Reform: Wittgenstein and Popper as Austrian Schoolmasters', in R. S. Cohen and M. W. Wartofsky (eds), *Method and Metaphysics* (Boston, 1974).
16. Cf. *On Certainty (Oxford 1974) s. 97.
17. See my *A Philosophical Approach to Religion* (London, 1974) ch. 6; 'What Makes Religious Beliefs Religious?', *Religious Studies*, vol. 13, 1977; and 'Theology and the Intellectual Endeavour of Mankind', *Religious Studies* (forthcoming).

8 Attitudes to Evidence and Argument in the Field of Religion

R. W. HEPBURN

I

The more a person's life is to be affected by some decision, and the more deeply affected, the greater his need to have learned good rational strategies that will help him to reach the best-supported of the options before him. If a student needs careful instruction in weighing up alternative words and phrases when translating from one language to another and in the devising of experiments to test hypotheses in science, he has still greater need for help in becoming able to cope rationally with the question of decision for or against an entire religious view, an ideology or a comprehensive speculative system. Young people are the constant targets of proselytising apologists for a very large range of conflicting views, for some of which a vastly stronger case can be made than for others. Yet though an alert critical vigilance and a capacity for clear-headed appraisal are so obviously important for discriminating among their claims, there exists a remarkable range of both religious and philosophical checks and impediments to developing and applying such appraisal.

A teacher or lecturer in the general area of religion is often uncomfortably aware of a conflict between the educational ideals operative in a very wide range of secular subjects and certain views about religious commitments held by some writers on the religions. If one is aiming to educate, not indoctrinate, at a moderately advanced level in – say – history, political theory, or in the sciences, one tries to show pupils not only how far particular proposed conclusions are grounded in evidence and how well-based in argument, but also how, more generally, to set about testing, confirming, falsifying *any* proposed conclusions in those fields. It may well be that the teacher himself is committed to a rational-critical principle, that assent to propositions should be regulated by the force of the evidence and the arguments in their support, and by the outcome of attempts to falsify them. He hopes to instil a similar attitude in his pupil; to further the pupil's intellectual autonomy.

Such aims, it might be supposed, could readily be carried across into the study of the religions and alternative systems of belief. Their objective would be to help the student himself to *choose well*, to choose, that is, the view most likely to be true. And the discriminating of true from false would necessarily be through a discriminating of better from worse argument and of more from less impressive evidence.

But then, turning to some important writings in the philosophy of religion, one may read sharply contrasting views. In most general terms, it may be argued that reason and rational testing procedures are altogether incompetent and inappropriate in the field of religion. To have the dimmest grasp of what is meant by divine transcendence or otherness is to see that it escapes, eludes our concepts and categories. Any being for whom we *did* have evidence and arguments would amount only to a 'god of the philosophers', an illusory construction of thought and imagination, irrelevant to religion.

It may be urged that the claims of religion are irreducible to metaphysical, speculative, rationally appraisable claims; and, for some writers, even a religion like Christianity that puts great stress on its historical narratives should not be daunted by the uncertainties and fluctuations of historical proof and disproof. We shall have to ask, however, whether a standpoint that does seek at all costs to avoid reducing the distinctively religious to the speculative and metaphysical, or indeed to the stories of history or pseudo-history, has intractable problems ahead of it. We may well suspect that it rests, itself, on implicit metaphysical foundations, for all its wish to be free of them. Its defenders, after all, still face the problem of discriminating among rival, incompatible accounts of transcendence, and indeed of God's acts in history. We have to ask, that is, whether either in the field of rational theology or historicity those claims about the distinctiveness and irreducibility of religion, impressive and influential as they are, do *fairly* deflect us from centring attention upon argument and evidence.

Other writers again may remind us that in any systematically ordered view of the world, religious or non-religious, not every item of belief can be 'derived' from some foundational or basic notion, premise or datum. The foundational components, whatever they are, cannot themselves be so derived. And, although philosophy may have tended to look, for such components, to 'atomic facts' or to sense-data, or to common-sense belief about the world of things and persons, some take *God* to be foundational. For those who do so, God will not feature as the conclusion of a rational case for belief in his existence.

There is another way still in which the same conclusion may be reached – namely that no reasoned case can successfully discriminate between different religious and non-religious views of the world. Different religions may be seen as so many alternative 'conceptual schemes' or 'conceptual frameworks' or 'language-games': and, it is said, we have no neutral or scheme-transcending concepts through which rationally to discriminate between such schemes. A language-game, wrote Wittgenstein, 'is not based on grounds. ... It is there – like our life'. Religious belief, Norman Malcolm claimed, paraphrasing Wittgenstein, 'does not rise or fall on the basis of evidence or grounds: it is "groundless"'.[1]

Lastly, the religions are often set forth, not as vouched for by reasoning and evidence, but as so many answers to primarily *practical* questions. How can human beings find fulfilment for their spiritual potentialities? How make available and stabilise that freedom from insecurity, that ultimate optimism, that thankfulness and assurance in the basic goodness of the world – all of them life-enhancing – which fugitive moments of religious experience may lure us into seeing as permanent possibilities, but are for the most part unrealised or undeveloped? Are there any grounds for inferring from the capacities of a religion to bring some kind of fulfilment to its believers, to the truth of that religion? Is it reasonable to conclude (as does H. A. Hodges in *God Beyond Knowledge*) that the ultimate 'real choice lies in an existential decision: which of the competing systems of beliefs and attitudes will the more fully liberate the deeper self'?[2] Can reliance upon 'pragmatic' factors rather than upon argument and evidence, be justifiable in some circumstances but not in others?

Here the agenda must end, though it could be substantially longer.

II

Consider, then, very briefly the first and extreme position where the divine object of religious concern is said so far to transcend human reason that the attempt to conduct a rational appraisal of religion is no more than an impertinence and irrelevance. Restricting our view to Christian theism, I would argue that this position cannot be consistently maintained. While insisting that our language can only very imperfectly characterise deity, Christians do nevertheless accept certain claims about the transcendent as less misleading or even nearer the truth than others: accepting e.g. that God is wholly and eternally good rather than partially or intermittently good, that he alone creates and maintains the world, and that beside him there are no other gods. Such preferences are intelligible, and, to a point, defensible. We are not here beyond the scope of reason. Christian religious claims can conflict with non-Christian metaphysical claims. They clash, for instance, with materialist or with monistic metaphysics. Metaphysical components then have to be acknowledged within Christian doctrine: the appraisal of those cannot be plausibly deemed irrelevant.

It is far from true that we must simply acknowledge a conflict of values, between the values of rational enquiry and the values of certain religious systems. It can be urged, moreover, that any anti-intellectualist persuasion is persuasion to discard the only guide we have in the complex task of discriminating between incompatible, rival sets of beliefs. Similarly, in a *moral* dispute, to attempt to persuade a person to set aside his conscience in favour of a would-be authority is to deprive him of his only moral guide, and amounts to corrupting him morally.

A robust reply could be expected to these points. The analogy could be accepted: the command of God can indeed be a command to suspend the human-ethical, and in the same way the revealed word of God can and does supplant fallible human efforts towards understanding the universe and our place in it.

Nothing, however, rules out a further question, namely, How do you know that this is how things stand? – that you correctly describe our situation *vis-à-vis* a self-revealing deity and a supra-rational message and system of values? Such claims, again, are highly vulnerable to error and illusion; more than one faith makes them, and so the need for renewed rational discrimination, for sifting of evidence and argument, is clear and inescapable. Before any limiting of rational appraisal can be taken seriously, and any appeal to supra-rational authority allowed, the authenticity of the authority, and the truth of the believer's account of his situation *vis-à-vis* the Transcendent, would have to be vindicated or at least made plausible.

Some writers would nonetheless argue that it is only by a subtle distortion or 'reduction' to a nature not their own that claims about God and belief in God are presented as *metaphysical* claims about a Mind with infinite power, knowledge, love. They will urge that between speculation and belief held in a truly religious way there is a great gulf fixed: and so again the argumentation and evidence-gathering that may go with the first is irrelevant to the second.

I should say again in response that although theistic religion is indeed not identical with metaphysical speculation, it nevertheless cannot be disentangled from metaphysics. Certainly, worship is not reflection upon ontology; yet the object of worship, if adequate, must possess some characteristics that can properly be the object of reflection and rational understanding. To acknowledge this cannot be fairly described as distorting religious claims. It is, rather, to imply that religion is many-levelled; and that some of those levels seemingly farthest from metaphysics (religious practices like prayer, praise, meditation, the Eucharist) may yet depend for their meaningfulness and efficacy upon that other level – the philosophical level – concerned to describe how the world is and what if anything transcends it. This is of course messy, and makes religious belief inescapably vulnerable to a philosophical critique. But what are the alternatives? One would be to hold to the distinctiveness, autonomy and irreducibility of religious concepts and claims, at whatever cost: so to emphasise God's transcendence or otherness as to make his existence or non-existence quite beyond argument and evidence. Such a move, however, at the same time attenuates and ultimately severs connections between Transcendence and the life of humanity, its hopes, needs and aspirations. Another alternative is to keep the connections, make religious language in effect practical and regulative, moral above all, and proclaim the foreignness or irrelevance of any cosmological and metaphysical reference to transcendent being. This amounts to a programme of demythologising, carried to the very foundations of Christian belief. In their virtual denial of the complexity – the many-levelled nature – of religion, it is these latter responses that distort and reduce the distinctively and complexly religious to something simpler but alien to religion. The first replaces traditional Christianity with a rarified religious agnosticism, and the second replaces it with a naturalism together with a set of action-guiding symbols. Neither captures or retains historical Christianity as such.

The most difficult versions to deal with critically and in an educational context are those that neither acknowledge a radical divergence from historical Christianity nor the relevance, for the assessing of their claims, of the arguments for and against God's existence or of the evidence and counter-evidence relating to Christian historical claims.

Wittgenstein was profoundly unsympathetic to argument, in the style say of Hume's *Dialogues*, on the existence of God. He was equally dismissive of debate over historical evidence. In *Culture and Value* he wrote: 'Christianity is not based on a historical truth; rather, it offers us a (historical) narrative and says: now believe! But not ... with the belief appropriate to a historical narrative, rather: believe, through thick and thin, ...'. And again: 'The historical accounts in the Gospels might, historically speaking, be demonstrably false and yet belief would lose nothing by this: *not*, however, because it concerns "universal truths of reason"! Rather, because historical proof (the historical proof-game) is irrelevant to belief.'[3]

The fact that a writer can indicate (as Wittgenstein does) modes of argument, types of evidence that he wants to dismiss as unsuitable for the religious matter-in-hand does not by itself show that there exists – coherent and certainty-conferring – some alternative, suitable view of the religion. As J. L. Mackie argued in *The Miracle of Theism*, we look in vain for such a clear *positive* account in Wittgenstein or in his more recent interpreters.[4] Since there exist rival, incompatible views, we have no option but to explore the strength or weakness of the *grounding* of the view we are examining. And the clarifying of purely internal connections within the circle of Christian concepts, important though that is, postpones the latter task: does not displace it.

If this is right (and some more argument will follow), the implications for education are these. It needs always to be taken into account (with students advanced enough to grasp the point) that the claims of a particular version of some religious view may possibly be confused. Its defenders may plausibly argue – for instance – that its concepts are not metaphysical, and that violence may be done to them by 'reducing' them to metaphysics. Yet it may be true that even to take it seriously *on its own terms* does presuppose the soundness of metaphysical presuppositions. The defender protests, understandably, against taking his distinctively religious beliefs on to the metaphysical plane; nevertheless, it may be only on that plane that key elements in them can be grounded and tested.

It must be allowed that it is for the most part precisely those levels farthest from metaphysics that engage most immediately with the believer's practical religious life, with his imaginative and emotional life also – as these are suffused with the symbolism of religion. In comparison with the devotion and religious feeling evoked by the latter, the concepts of metaphysics may be denied to be part of religion at all. They can, nevertheless, be entirely necessary fundamental presuppositions for the belief that there exists any real object corresponding to the intentional object of our emotions, any being before whom alone our 'responses' of gratitude, hope and trust will prove to be appropriate. (Compare the situation in science. Not everything the scientist crucially relies on is itself 'science': neither his instrument-readings nor the necessary truths of the mathematics he uses are 'science'; nevertheless they are in different ways indispensable to his doing science at all.)

Even so, the other side of this matter needs more emphasis than I have allowed it so far. Anyone who is at all sensitive to religious experience knows how strong the impulse can be to declare the domain of religion autonomous, its responses and forms of awareness *sui generis* and therefore quite beyond the reach of its philosophical critics. Leszek Kolakowski argued that both our elemental experience of being and not-being, and religious faith based on revelation, 'suffer a deep corruption when they are articulated in the idioms of philosophical and theological speculation ...'.[5] Certainly for a person who has known or glimpsed some of the forms of *mystical* experience even in the most partial fashion, it is not an affectation or mere convention to claim that any conceptualizing of the experience fails drastically to capture its quality. True, he may allow himself to talk about it, knowing that no talk does more than stammer and approximate. But if some direct experiential reminder should then come to him again, he may well say, 'My words have utterly missed their target: to say that they "approximate" is far too generous a judgement on them.' And if the descriptions all fail, even more will the words of criticism be off the point. There exists an incommensurability between certain forms of religious or mystical experience and the experiences of everyday which language is well-tailored to record. An aesthetic analogy is in order again. A programme-note cannot evoke, in advance of a performance of a piece of music, the exact emotional qualities of the music itself: they are distinctively musical and not verbalisable qualities.

Do not these remarks signal an about-turn, a willingness after all to allow what I have so far been refusing to allow – an appeal to the distinctiveness of the religious, and the consequent irrelevance of philosophical and historical criticism? No: the qualitative distinctiveness of mystical experience and its incommensurability with experience of other kinds, although it may block sceptical dismissal and entitle that experience to a lastingly impressive place among human experiences generally, still cannot by itself establish its *cognitive* status: cannot tell us, that is, whether or not it is a *bona fide* revelation of how things ultimately stand. The aesthetic analogy could here be appealed to by the sceptic: qualitatively distinctive, unique *musical* emotion does not, on account of that character alone, acquire a cognitive authority. Moreover some people have experiences, awake or in dream, of an ultimately *malign* cosmic power; and such quasi-satanic revelations can be as stunningly convincing to the subject as their beatific counterparts. That our fallibility extends through the whole range of religious experiences seems to me the only conclusion.

I should repeat that, altough the matter cannot be opened up here, the denial of cognitive, revelatory standing to mystical experience of certain kinds does not necessarily destroy the importance of such experience. J. L. Mackie argues in *The Miracle of Theism* that such a devaluation is likely, on a non-cognitive interpretation.[6] But a naturalist could nevertheless consistently attach high value to those experiential transformations of his world, marvelling at the fact that the human agent and his environment conspire to produce such utterly counterintuitive modes of consciousness, and taking seriously their bearing on the moral life also. What educational implications flow from all this?

Because the cognitive status of religious and mystical experience is so indeterminate, there is no option but to look to any possible aids to resolving that issue, or at least giving some likelihood to one interpretation over the other. In other words, questions of evidence and argument, historical and philosophical, have not been shown irrelevant – even by the phenomena of incommensurability and qualitative uniqueness in episodic religious experience.

A difficult balance is called for (by the teacher) between, on the one side, respect for testimony about episodes of personal religious experience, and, on the other side, an encouraging of critical alertness towards any cognitive claims based on such experience. Nothing is easier than to ironically disparage a pupil's potentiality for personal religious experience, before it has had any chance to be maturely reflected upon. (Indeed, such experience may all too readily, and without argument, come to be taken as immature in its essential nature!) Nevertheless, a proper respect for the pupil's experience should not be over-extended to the point of implying that experience brings with it its infallible interpretation. To achieve that balance is not, of course, merely a strategy for the teacher, but is a main part of what he may encourage his pupils to adopt autonomously as their own strategy for sorting out their individual experience in religion. Rather than espousing either sort of dogmatism – of belief or unbelief – a student may well suffer less harm if left poised *between* belief and disbelief. On the one side is belief in a God who could indeed only be stammered at, since if he exists his nature is immeasurably different from any of our more or less conceptualised, determinate ideas of greatness. Whatever we do grasp cannot be God. (Compare Anselm, *Proslogion*, chapter 15.) And on the other side – the surmise is that the experience causally results from a complex interaction between the psyche (conscious and unconscious) and its widest grasping of nature: no transcendents being involved.

III

For some believers the existence of God is not the subject of proofs and counterproofs and the weighing of evidence, since it is part of what they count as basic or foundational. *Something*, they say, must have that status: God may have it. Alvin Plantinga describes such a view:

> The mature believer [he writes] ... does not typically accept belief in God ... as a conclusion from other things he believes; he accepts it as basic, as a part of the foundations of his noetic structure. The mature theist *commits* himself to believe in God; this means that he accepts belief in God as basic ... there is nothing contrary to reason or irrational in so doing.[7]

Plantinga first considers 'classical foundationalism'. Essential to this is the claim not only that knowledge has a structure, articulated from the 'basic' to the derived and inferred, but also that basic beliefs must be 'self-evident' or 'incorrigible'. Several problems lead Plantinga to reject classical foundationalism. A *seemingly* self-evident proposition may be deceptive: Russell's paradoxes taught that lesson dramatically. ('... from propositions that seem self-evident, [we deduce] ... by arguments that seem self-evidently right, that non-self-exemplification both exemplifies itself and does not exemplify itself.'[8]) If instead we try: 'Whatever seems self-evident is very likely true', we have the new problem of justifying *that* claim. Even if it were itself deemed self-evident, that would be a reason for judging it true, only if we had already good grounds for accepting what it says – i.e. the very proposition we are trying to justify. The case is worse still when we consider the other requirement of the classical foundationalist for 'basic' status: that *only* self-evident or incorrigible propositions are properly basic. The proposition which affirms that requirement is itself neither self-evident nor incorrigible, even though it must function as basic to the classical foundationalist. Having shown the 'self-referential incoherence' of classical foundationalism, Plantinga hopes he has paved the way to a foundationalism that the theist can adopt and which the mature theist does characteristically adopt: one in which belief in God is itself among the foundations, despite the fact that it could not plausibly be basic to classical foundationalism.

Does not this, however, amount to saying that belief in God is 'groundless', 'arbitrary'? No: just as 'I see a tree' can be basic and yet justified by my present experience 'together with other circumstances', so too belief in God can be both basic (not derived from reasoning and weighing of evidence) and grounded. 'God has so created us that we have a disposition to see his hand in the world about us'. Plantinga claims there are 'many conditions and circumstances that call forth belief in God': they include 'guilt, gratitude, danger, a sense of God's presence'.[9]

What Plantinga wishes to call 'basic' is, however, a reading of experience that (although it is certainly not presented as a formally *argued* and *evidence-backed* position) can nevertheless be challenged or denied by defenders of alternative readings. Readings are not beyond the reach of reason, in support or in criticism. From the fact that we have a 'disposition' to read the world one way rather than another, we cannot infer that this way leads to true belief: it might have survival value (and so be advantageous in evolutionary terms) and yet be untrue.[10] It is at any rate subject to possible correction and needs to be exposed to such correction. In tension with my intuitive pre-critical disposition to see God's hand in the living world may be set the Darwinian hypotheses that account for adaptation without positing purpose or design. Again, what *historical* events seem to me to show God's hand most dramatically will depend on my beliefs about what actually *happened* on the occasions that interest me; hence my 'reading' of God's actions in history is intimately dependent on my view of the evidence for what occurred (e.g. at the Exodus, on the third day after the crucifixion of Jesus or at the alleged Ascension). In a word, the concern with argument and evidence, that seemed to be displaced by a view that takes belief in God as basic, has not by any means been shown irrelevant or misguided. Plantinga's provision of 'grounds' for the basic belief turns out to be continuous with the rational construction-and-criticism and sifting of evidence.

If a believer accepts the argument just offered, accepts that it is possible to challenge and contest a 'reading' or interpretation, and yet remains a foundationalist, that can only mean that he has taken a decision – not to enter the debate over alternative readings, not to reconsider the question whether his own reading is mistaken. Implications for education do seem to follow from this: namely that a teacher or a writer in religious studies and philosophy of religion should acknowledge that although the status of being 'basic' is claimed by some theists for their belief in God, that does not (as Plantinga allows) rule out 'God exists' having grounds. But if the experiences and considerations that make up those grounds are examined seriously, it cannot be denied that they can be construed in more ways than one. It can be argued that the 'intricate universe' demands no maker, nor my sense of forgiveness any actual divine Forgiver. Only *will* can prevent disputes over these and other 'grounds' from joining up again with the whole continuum of philosophical–theological argument.

We need to spell out more fully the principle on which this criticism of a 'foundationalist' theism rests. If we are concerned to discover the truth of some matter and to open the way to others' discovery of it also, we should work with the policy of never holding any content of belief to be above argument or removed from the assessment of evidence for and against it, so long as reason can get any foothold at all. More particularly, since burying some challengeable, fallible contention in the foundations of my belief-structure *does* remove it from scrutiny and reassessment, it is educationally bad to give approval to such a move – a move by which strenuous apologetics are replaced by the claim, 'Oh, but for me that's basic!' There are reasonable alternatives to theism, and indeed a variety of *prima facie* objections to it. Reason *can* get a foothold; therefore it must be allowed to do so. Wherever a rational case *could* be made to assess the plausibility of any view, a case *should* be made, and the foundational, privileged status abandoned.

It is on similar lines that I should wish to respond to Leszek Kolakowski in his book, *Religion*.

> Everything ultimately goes back [he wrote] to the basic principle: trust God ... [Trust is] given *a priori*.

... why should anybody trust God or admit His existence at all? If 'why' means 'on what grounds similar to those we refer to in accepting scientific hypotheses?' there is no answer, as there are no grounds of this kind. But the question may be reversed: what reasons can be adduced for holding that the rules normally followed in testing and in provisionally accepting scientific hypotheses define ... the limits of what is meaningful or acceptable? Or: what are the grounds of scientific rationalism?[11]

We should readily concede that the methodology of science does not circumscribe the 'meaningful' and the 'acceptable'. But once we do show willingness to admit as meaningful, and as candidates for acceptance, non-scientific speculative and religious claims, the result is the admission of not one but indefinitely many candidate views. Unless we relinquish freedom and reason and allow the sheer contingencies of our upbringing and its religious climate and context to determine our particular allegiance, we cannot, again, evade the task of discrimination, the finding of grounds for trusting in God under *this* description rather than *that* description, for *trusting* in God rather than being *wary* of him, for trusting in one God rather than in two or two hundred.

> Philosophical investigation [Kolakowski writes] is forever unable to produce, to replace, or even to encourage the act of faith. ... This is not to say that the questions surrounding the philosophers' God are uninteresting or flimsy; they are simply irrelevant to what Christianity or any religion is about. Whether this God exists or not is hardly a religious issue, and is not a real worry to people to whom such issues matter.[12]

Kolakowski sees 'philosophical investigation' as sharply contrasted with 'acts of faith'. The really important point for comment is not the empirical question of whether philosophical reflection does, as a matter of fact, result in faith or loss of faith. (On that, anyway, I am sure Kolakowski is wrong: there are individuals, in my own experience, whose faith is disturbed, and others whose faith is confirmed by reflecting on arguments for and against God's existence.) But the question for us here is: *ought* they to take such considerations to heart? Or can faith (again) be foundational and thus not a conclusion of any reflective process? One could of course say Yes to the last question, if there were in fact a clear, sharp distinction between the

God of the philosophers and the God of the religious, so that the one was indeed irrelevant to the other. But the whole trend of my argument in this chapter is that this view, though commonly held, cannot be sustained. Nothing is more central to the religious conception of God than the idea of maximal worship-worthiness. If God were shown to lack certain characteristics, his worship-worthiness would be impaired: that is to say, his religious role would be decisively affected. But among these characteristics are omnipotence, omniscience, eternal mode of being, infinite goodness: all of them concepts of the utmost concern to the philosopher of religion, whose conclusions in respect of them are therefore inescapably relevant to the religious believer or would-be believer. How misleading to say: 'Whether the philosophers' God exists or not is hardly a religious issue.' In a word, no matter how psychologically strong the believer's conviction about God may be, or how little heed he takes of the arguments for and against God's existence and nature, these issues remain highly disputable in fact: and that is sufficient reason not to accord theistic belief 'basic' or 'foundational' status.

It is sometimes argued that, from a religious point of view, there is insufficient security or peace of mind in a religious belief derived (with more or less probability) from argument or evidence. But it seems to me that in matters of high complexity and intellectual boldness – such as the affirming of God's 'infinite' attributes – total epistemic security cannot be had. Nor, it must be said again, is appeal to revelation any remedy, since the same insecurity attends the acceptance of texts and persons as having divine authority or authenticity. The educator, far from being abashed in his emphasis upon evidence and argument, should surely make it one of his aims to help pupils to *live with*, and not be paralysed by, that insecurity, nor again self-deceivingly evade it. They need help to make their own best interpretation and to hold it with the degree of confidence that is reasonable, but with a continuing sense also of their fallibility.

IV

We must now consider the implications of that highly general epistemological model, which (in simplified forms) has been very widely influential and entails important limitations upon appeals to argument and evidence. It is the view that there exist indefinitely many conceptual or linguistic frameworks or schemes and that justification and criticism can go on only within a particular scheme, since the justificatory and critical activities themselves are always relative, or internal, to one or other conceptual scheme. The religions of the world are such conceptual schemes. The model has been very understandably attractive to some students of comparative religion who seek to escape from a domineering scientism or positivism. So many religious views, so many conceptual schemes, picture-preferences.

Even so, the attractiveness is limited. Taken to the letter, such a thought-model excludes any criticism of any self-styled religion, whether on metaphysical or even on moral grounds. Any seeming-incoherence has to be seen as idiosyncratic logic, and any apparent moral perversity as, simply, its distinctive moral norms. Rather than accept the model, however, it might be thought more reasonable to take these implications of it as a *reductio ad absurdum*: that is to say, if not even the most bizarre cult has anything to fear from a philosophical critique, hospitability may have gone absurdly far, and the underlying thought-model is due to be rejected. In any case, there are other grounds for rejecting the model. The only circumstances in which there would indeed be no possibility of rational assessment across conceptual schemes are where the conceptual schemes are distinct from one another in a very strong sense. At the limit, they would not have concepts (or beliefs) in common; they would employ quite different categories of thought, and the languages expressing their views of the world would be untranslatably different. Indeed, neither could be identified *as* language by the other.[13] This, however, is very far from being the case with the languages and concepts of, say, Judaism, Theravada Buddhism, Confucianism, Catholic Christianity and atheistic materialism. If it were the case, then obviously no education would be possible in this field. Clearly these are distinct and different conceptual frameworks only in a much weaker, looser sense. But to loosen the sense is to allow that there is some overlap of categories and other concepts among them; and there is indeed a very substantial overlap, despite some real divergences.

It is true and important that key expressions in any religious view will be in some measure affected – in their nuances, resonance, implications – by linguistic oppositions and affinities with other key terms within that same view. But it does not follow that the whole meaning of these expressions is internally determined. For instance, the concept of 'the world' in Christian theology is internally related to such concepts as the work of creation, contingency and derivativeness: but it does not follow that we can give no sense to a dispute between Christian and non-Christian on whether the world is dependent upon God or enjoys an eternal and uncreated existence. There is still enough common meaning to make that dispute possible. By no means all the linguistic relations are internal to the system: the systems are not sealed or insulated from one another. A materialist and a theist share the categories of substance, event, causality, agency, of validity and invalidity in argument, and many more – enough to make ludicrous the claim that there is no work for reason in weighing up their respective conflicting opinions about God. In opposing this still very seductive model, we add to the scope of rational deliberation in the appraisal of world views and religions. To reject it is, also, to remove one justification for allowing place to pragmatic considerations in deciding religious commitment: so the present topic is closely connected with our final one.

The distinction just made – between the correct claim that religious concepts have numerous internal relations with other concepts in the same religious view, and the incorrect claim that *all* strands of their meaning are internal – carries one far-reaching implication. It is only if the second claim is accepted that issues like God's goodness or his forgiveness become matters of 'grammar'. Only by such a move is the question, for instance, of 'eternal life' denied to be a philosophical issue continuous with philosophers' discussions of personal identity, mind and body etc. However internally well-connected is the concept of 'eternal life' with neighbouring religious concepts, so long as it concerns the continuation, in some mode of being, of individual existence beyond death, questions of identity cannot fail to engage with it. The alternative, which ought to be explicit, not mysteriously implicit, is a thoroughgoing demythologizing of the idea – in this-worldly moral and existential terms. No doubt there are hints in biblical writings of such a possible treatment, but thoroughgoing they are not.

V

I turn, finally, to consider, briefly, the logic of pragmatic defences of religious claims. Supposing it can be shown that a particular set of beliefs offers unique prospects of fulfilling the moral and religious aspirations of a person who commits himself to it, and that it comprises a framework of ideas that interprets, stabilises and unifies what are otherwise fugitive and elusive episodes of religious experience. Suppose it offers a view of the universe that is not at all alien to the conception of the subject-self as a spiritual being. It vindicates, rather than reduces to absurdity, his spiritual struggles. Factors of this kind may, under certain circumstances, be taken to count, perhaps decisively to count, as grounds for religious commitment. The basis of such a pragmatic defence may be argued for, or (as is often the case) may be implicit only, in the presenting of a religious position.

In his essay, 'The Utility of Religion', J. S. Mill claimed that one may hold without contradiction that 'nature and life' are the 'product of a struggle between contriving goodness and an intractable material'. A morally serious person may look on himself as a 'fellow-labourer with the Highest': that is to say with a good, though (for Mill) finite deity. The evidence for such a deity was no more than 'shadowy and insubstantial'. It 'cannot' however 'be known to be false'; so we may legitimately meditate upon these possibilities, 'feeding and animating the tendency of the feelings and impulses towards good'.[14] In *The Will to Believe*, William James claimed that 'our passional nature not only lawfully may, but must, decide an option between propositions, whenever it is a genuine option that cannot by its nature be decided on intellectual grounds ...'. The claims apply only to cases where reasoned support and criticism are inconclusive, and no more work can be done with them.[15]

There, however, is the rub. Is it really credible that in the field we are considering, one could ever know that that point had been reached – that the evidence and counter-evidence had been finally sifted, considered from every possible angle and in every light, and that none of the arguments could be further re-interpreted, sharpened, or shown to have hitherto-unnoticed flaws? If we do *not* reach that point, on the other hand, we lack entitlement to allow the desirable practical aspects of the doctrines to count as grounds for believing that the doctrines are *true*. 'A belief can be a condition of life,' wrote Nietzsche, 'and nonetheless be false.' 'Among the conditions of life might be error.'[16] These are hard sayings, because there is no question about the animating, life-enhancing character of many religious ideas and experiences – summed up perhaps as a sense of vital participation in a life that far, and gloriously, transcends one's own. Many theists may agree with H. A. Hodges that 'one chooses that belief which allows expression to one's authentic self', and that 'in the mystery we find escape from finitude, even from our own finitude, and satisfaction of our impulse towards self-transcendence'.[17] But Nietzsche's austere words need to be recalled if anyone is tempted vaguely to imagine that a belief has already passed the test of truth precisely in being shown to have animating and liberating powers. To put it another way: unless I can already rely on a view of the world as in the hand of a caring Providence, I have no grounds for assurance that what expresses my authentic self, what lets me shake off my sense of finitude, *matches* the way the world ultimately is.

Suppose I interpret my religious experience as experience of being in 'harmony' with the world, a condition signalled by a sense of well-being. But now, unless I can rely also upon a *non*-pragmatically justified metaphysic, how do I know that I am *in fact* harmoniously interacting with a world to which I am sensitively attuned? May I not, rather, be obtaining my religious 'peak-experience' by heeding a highly selected *sample* of the world's signals, and blocking all the rest? Perhaps I am not, as I imagined, opening myself to ultimate reality, but *shutting off* most of it from awareness? To rule out that possibility, I need metaphysical licence that cannot itself be only pragmatically warranted. I cannot 'help myself' to the belief that whatever conditions are necessary to my functioning at my peak or being religiously fulfilled are indeed also fundamental features of the world. This essential and sober distinction between, on the one hand, truth, and, on the other hand power to fulfil, surely needs honest discussion in courses of religious studies.

Throughout this chapter I have been urging that, in the absence of convincing counter-reasons, the assent we are entitled to give to a set of claims in the field of religion should be appropriate to the strength of the arguments and evidence relevant to its truth. That basic rational-critical principle generates educational strategies – relating both to the manner in which a teacher should present disputable religious and philosophical theses to pupils (at moderately advanced levels, we are assuming), and to the methods of assessment the pupils are encouraged, themselves, to pursue. We have briefly considered, and rejected, a number of pleas, within philosophy of religion, that the principle should not be taken to apply to certain sorts of religious claim. I have not entered the debate on the status and possible justification of the principle itself.[18]

I am very far from thinking that the status of the rationalistic principle is unproblematic or unchallengeable by more sophisticated forms of 'pragmatic' outlook than I have considered here. This cannot be properly considered in the present chapter. One comment only may be ventured.

There may well be something odd, logically, about the demand to provide a justification for the principle that, *prima facie*, assent to a proposition ought to be given in proportion to 'the strength of the logically relevant evidence for its truth'. The demand is a demand for justification, the principle being called to the bar of reason – among, we must imagine, other possible principles. But the principle we are considering just *is* the principle that we bring claims-to-our-credence before the bar of reason, and believe them to the extent that their pleas succeed. To reject *it* is to dismantle the bar of reason: in other words, the rationalistic principle is *presupposed* by any practice of bringing principles before the bar of reason. We can show concern, i.e. about how the rationalistic principle can or cannot be justified, only if we are already committed to it, and thus are concerned with reasons and evidence in general. To turn away from it is to reject the life of reason; though I doubt if we could reject the life of reason consistently and thoroughly. (This is all quite compatible with acknowledging exceptions, e.g. the acceptance of pragmatic considerations where argument and evidence are indeed balanced and inconclusive.)

Do not people adduce in debate, however, in addition to the general intellectual considerations that we have so far inquired into, some much more specifically religious factors relevant to the managing of their commitments and critical reappraisals of the religions themselves? A theistic believer may say, for instance, that believing and disbelieving, are, for him, equivalent to either trusting in a divine Person or faltering and failing in that person-to-person relation. To see his situation in that way certainly puts rather different constraints upon him than if he saw himself as appraising and reappraising a scientific theory or a legal judgment or an interpretation of a poem. Serious critical appraisal of a religion may be termed 'doubt' and doubt construed as reprehensible loss of nerve, or trust, or even incipient betrayal of one's religious tradition and fellow-believers.

I shall not rehearse the factors that lead to this latter view. I do think however that there are good reasons for refusing to accept it as equally fundamental and therefore directly in opposition to the approach I have so far outlined in this paper. It already presupposes that the believer does indeed stand overagainst a divine Person, that his situation is correctly interpreted in those terms, and that therefore personal-relation concepts and value-judgements are appropriate in describing his misgivings and doubt. Clearly, these presuppositions themselves are the really fundamental target for appraisal and critical reappraisal.

Thrown into relief here is something that the teacher of religion should certainly be aware of, and help his pupils to become aware of – the self-protective devices a religion may sometimes use in order to discourage its believers from questioning its basic claims. Similar devices may operate with potential, as well as established, believers. For a religion that seeks to attract converts by immersing newcomers and 'enquirers' in a 'fellowship' of intense loving concern, the rejecting of the religion's beliefs may be presented as undistinguishable from the rejecting of that love – something that is psychologically extremely difficult to its recipient, and immediately arouses guilt.

What can be conceded is that a policy of constant, sustained and intense critical onslaught against his own fundamental beliefs would prevent any one from participating at all effectively in the way of life appropriate to those beliefs, and in consort with others who share them. Practical wisdom in this area, for teacher and taught, requires finding a mean, between on the one side such a relentless self-critical campaign, and on the other a complacent, or an over-anxious, refusal ever to reappraise.[19]

NOTES

1. L. Wittgenstein, *On Certainty* (Oxford: Blackwell, 1974), §559; also S. C. Brown (ed.), *Reason and Religion*, (Ithaca and London, Cornell University Press, 1977) p. 148.
2. H. A. Hodges, *God Beyond Knowledge* (London: The Macmillan Press Ltd., 1979) p. 173.
3. L. Wittgenstein, *Culture and Value* (Oxford: Blackwell, 1980) p. 32.
4. J. L. Mackie, *The Miracle of Theism* (Oxford: Clarendon Press, 1982) esp. ch. 12.
5. L. Kolakowski, *Religion* (Fontana, 1982) p. 74.
6. J. L. Mackie, op. cit., pp. 186–7, and ch. 12.
7. A. Plantinga, 'Is Belief in God Rational?', in C. F. Delaney (ed.), *Rationality and Religious Belief* (University of Notre Dame Press, 1979). pp. 7–27. See also Plantinga's contribution to S. Cahn and Shatz (eds), *Contemporary Philosophy of Religion*, (New York: Oxford University Press 1982) pp. 255–77.
8. Cahn and Shatz, op. cit., pp. 259–70.
9. Ibid., pp. 272–3: Plantinga considers objections to his thesis on pp. 270–7.
10. Cf. below, pp. 141–5.

11. L. Kolakowski, op. cit., pp. 47–50.
12. Ibid., pp. 54, 67.
13. Very relevant is B. Stroud, 'Conventionalism and Translation', in D. Davidson and J. Hintikka (eds), *Words and Objections*, Dordrecht, D. Reidel, 1969, pp. 82–96. See also R. Rorty, *Consequences of Pragmatism* (Brighton: Harvester Press, 1982) ch. 1, 'The World Well Lost'.
14. J. S. Mill, 'The Utility of Religion', in *Three Essays on Religion*, pp. 116–8.
15. W. James, *The Will to Believe* (London: Longmans Green, 1897) p. 11.
16. F. Nietzsche, *The Will to Power*, trans. W. Kaufmann and R. J. Hollingdale (New York, Vintage Books, 1968) §483; *The Gay Science*, §121.
17. H. A. Hodges, *God Beyond Knowledge*, pp. 96–7, 175. Hodges, like Mill and James, claims that 'no decision can be made between the rival faiths on rational grounds' (p. 175).
18. The principle is interestingly discussed, and claimed to need (at least) qualification, in G. L. Doore, 'William James and the Ethics of Belief', *Philosophy*, vol. 58, 1983, pp. 353–64.
19. (a) None of the above should be taken to imply that I imagine pupils in early years of Religious Education as capable of rationally 'appraising' a set of religious beliefs, or that (for any age) appraisal should take precedence over learning and gaining a sympathetic understanding of a religion.

    (b) Nothing in the chapter indicates adequately the complexity and difficulty of the task of appraising a religious view. To do so was not my objective: but silence should not be taken to imply that I see that task as unproblematic. Much (and at some levels and in some contexts probably all) of an instructor's efforts here may be towards rebutting premature dismissals of religious claims, and showing how particular criticisms may be met from within the religious view concerned.

9 Moral Development as the Goal of Moral Education

DON LOCKE

It is a tribute to the richness of Kohlberg's theory of moral development that it straddles the three disciplines of psychology, philosophy and education in a way which is, in my experience, unique. I have discussed some of the psychological and philosophical claims elsewhere (Locke, 1979, 1980, 1985); in this chapter I want to look at their practical application in the sphere of moral education. It can hardly be doubted that the approach which Kohlberg and his associates have developed provides a valuable educational tool, in ways which extend well beyond its specifically moral application. But Kohlberg has also argued that moral development, as he conceives it, should be the goal of moral education, that moral development provides a rationale and a justification for moral education, and that moral education should therefore be directed primarily at the development of moral reasoning, rather than, for example, the improvement of moral conduct or the teaching of moral standards.

I shall begin by outlining Kohlberg's original conception of moral education and its theoretical rationale. I shall then consider four possible reasons for regarding the development of moral reasoning in particular as the prime and proper goal of moral education. I shall argue that the case is neither so strong nor so exclusive as Kohlberg suggests: moral development, in his sense, may be *a* goal of moral education, of a rather limited sort; but it is not, on the evidence so far available, *the* goal. Finally I shall look at the way in which Kohlberg has subsequently revised his conception of moral education, a way which amounts, in effect, to abandoning moral development as its goal.

I

There are two important respects in which Kohlberg's approach to moral education departs from the current orthodoxy. Both stem from his cognitive-developmental theory of moral development, and in particular the claim that the different forms of moral reasoning represent increasingly more adequate ways of handling moral claims and conflicts. According to Kohlberg's theory (1969, 1971b, 1976), the moral thinking of children, teenagers and adults develops through a Piagetian sequence of six cognitive stages, each stage identified by a distinctive form of moral understanding and reasoning. These six stages are identified not by the particular moral judgements which people make, or the moral decisions they come to, but by the sorts of reason which they use to support or justify their judgements and decisions, and the understanding or comprehension of morality which that indicates. Thus different individuals may have differing moral opinions and yet be at the same stage of moral reasoning because they use similar sorts of consideration to justify their different opinions. As Kohlberg would put it, the content of their moral thinking may differ, but its form or structure is the same.

Moreover what moves the individual on from one stage, or form, of moral thinking to another, Kohlberg suggests, is cognitive conflict: that is, problems arising within a particular style of moral thinking which cannot be resolved within that mode of moral thought. A need for cognitive consistency, or what Kohlberg describes in Piagetian terms as an equilibration of accommodation and assimilation, accordingly moves the individual on to other, 'higher', stages of moral thinking, in which the problems arising at lower stages are satisfactorily resolved. In other words the suggestion is that at any particular stage in his development the individual will have a certain way of handling his moral experience, the claims and conflicts which the society of other people imposes on him. But new experiences, or more complex social interactions, or a more sophisticated perception of what those interactions involve, may generate claims and conflicts which he cannot resolve in the accustomed way, and he will therefore be forced to develop a more sophisticated and more effective method of handling his moral environment, and so move to a higher stage of moral reasoning. We thus have an explanation not merely of why people move from stage to stage at all, but of why they develop through these particular stages in this particular order.

The first consequence of this is that insofar as higher stages of reasoning are cognitively superior to lower stages, they will also be morally superior: since the higher stages are better able to reconcile moral claims and resolve moral conflicts, they are therefore to be preferred morally as well. Thus

> the scientific theory as to why people factually *do* move upward from stage to stage, and why they factually *do* prefer a higher stage to a lower, is broadly the same as a moral theory why people *should* prefer a higher stage to a lower. ... The logical relations between stages represent indifferently the structure of an adequate theory of moral judgment development, or the structure of an adequate theory as to why one system of moral judgment is better than another. (Kohlberg 1971a, p. 223-4)

Kohlberg is not here arguing that the later stages of moral development are superior to the earlier just because they occur later, much less that prescriptive moral judgements can somehow be reduced to descriptive psychological ones. But he is arguing that once we understand why one form of moral reasoning is developmentally superior to another, we will see that it is morally superior as well. In this way, he suggests, we can 'commit the Naturalistic Fallacy and get away with it'; we can, after all, move from an 'is' to an 'ought'.

Now the alleged autonomy of morals has made it almost an article of faith among theorists of moral education that the teaching of value should teach no particular values. Instead children might be taught the implications and commitments of various value positions, leaving the choice between those positions open; or they might be helped to clarify the values which they themselves already endorse, and in the process perhaps come to modify them; or they might be taught how to reason coherently about any matter of value, irrespective of the particular values they happen to subscribe to; or they might be taught the essential implications and commitments of any value position whatsoever, the inescapable logical and practical implications of moral discourse itself; or they might be taught certain fundamental values believed necessary for any rational morality whatever, while still allowing some degree of variability in the content of particular rational moralities. But if, as Kohlberg believes, it can be shown that some forms of moral thinking are indeed superior to others, cognitively and therefore morally, then it seems clear that the aim of moral education must be moral development: to bring as many children as possible as quickly as possible to as high a level of moral reasoning as possible.

But here we must take account of the second important consequence of Kohlberg's theory, that moral development of this sort is not something that can be achieved simply by instruction. The traditional approach to moral education was to inculcate what Kohlberg calls 'a bag of virtues', certain specific rules and values. But this is inadequate both morally and psychologically: morally because there will always be conflicts and special cases where particular rules have to be modified or abandoned; psychologically because merely laying down some approved mode of conduct does nothing to improve the individual's level of moral understanding. But the more contemporary approach, of attempting to train children in moral thinking as such, is equally inadequate, in as much as it appears that people typically have difficulty in comprehending moral reasoning at stages above their own, which they tend to reinterpret in terms of the lower-stage reasoning which they do understand. So we must seek to improve moral reasoning not by preaching, nor by teaching, but by cognitive stimulation: by bringing the individual into contact with those experiences which he can resolve and reconcile only by moving to the next stage of moral reasoning, and then to the next, and so on.

In practice this seems to involve two things, cognitive conflict, or the production of contradictions or uncertainties in the individual's own form of moral reasoning, and exposure to the next higher stage of reasoning which thus provides the individual with a new form of thinking with which to solve his difficulties. Accordingly Kohlberg and his associates have utilised two practical techniques in which these twin aims of inducing cognitive conflict and exposure to higher stages can combine to produce movement from one stage to the next. The first is what Kohlberg terms 'a Socratic process of discussion and disagreement': children are presented with moral problems, and encouraged to state and clarify their own solutions, and the reasoning which leads them to it; if that in itself does not produce cognitive conflict and at least some examples of reasoning at the next level, the instructor can then play Devil's Advocate, not by offering reasoning at his own level, but by pitching his arguments one stage higher than that of the majority of the class. This gives an interesting, and I have no doubt profitable, content to that part of the school timetable headed 'Moral Education', but there is of course no reason why the open discussion of moral, social and political questions should not be encouraged equally in other parts of the curriculum, wherever they naturally arise. Yet the second technique applies even more widely, and can be adopted in institutions other than schools, e.g. prisons.

This is what Kohlberg calls the 'just community' approach, i.e. self-regulation on the basis of open discussion and majority decision. These open discussions provide a further application of the Socratic technique; the fact that the decisions personally affect both the individual and his friends encourages the role-taking, or ability to see things from other people's points of view, which is crucial to moral development; and the moral atmosphere of the institution may itself expose the individual to a higher, more satisfactory and more satisfying, form of moral thinking.

Of course these two techniques are hardly original to Kohlberg and his associates, but in their work they do have a solid theoretical rationale and a concrete aim. Moreover the evidence from classroom studies is that students engaged in Socratic discussions do move to higher stages of moral reasoning faster than do those in control groups (Blatt and Kohlberg, 1975). The evidence from the just community experiments is less clearcut, inasmuch as Kohlberg tends to fasten on advantages which are independent of the cognitive-developmental theory – that it encourages a better sense of community, facilitates rehabilitations, and the like (Kohlberg *et al.*, 1975) – and any improvement in the level of moral reasoning cannot be directly due to the fact that the institution itself is organised according to Stage 6 principles, since according to the theory people have difficulty in understanding reasoning more than one stage above their own, and the predominantly Stage 2 and 3 members of the community should therefore consistently misunderstand and misinterpret those principles in terms which they do understand. Nevertheless there seems no reason why the open discussion of moral issues should not improve the level of moral reasoning in prisons as well as in schools. It is, after all, precisely what you would expect: practice, they say, makes perfect; no doubt the best way to improve your moral thinking is to engage in a bit from time to time.

But this brings us to the crux of the matter. What exactly is the aim of moral education: the improvement of moral *reasoning* or the improvement of moral *conduct*? The two are different, of course, and there is no obvious guarantee that the one will lead to the other. Indeed the cynical will expect the very reverse: that the more sophisticated an individual's moral thinking, the more sophistical it is liable to be; that given man's enormous capacity for hypocrisy, self-deception and special pleading, the more adept he will be at finding some way of avoiding those claims and duties which happen not to suit his private concerns and interests. Tolstoy, for one, thought that a simple moral consciousness is more likely to be pure and holy than a cerebral one, and who is to say he was wrong? We need, therefore, to notice the crucial ambiguity of the term 'moral development'. To suggest that moral development should be the goal of moral education seems almost a truism, if by 'moral development' we mean the development of moral conduct. But if we mean, as Kohlberg does, the development of moral reasoning, the claim is no longer so obvious.

Of course it is always possible to argue that since all values are relative, or at least incapable of objective or rational proof, moral education should concern itself not with altering people's behaviour but with improving their ability to handle moral questions in accordance with whatever values they happen to hold. Kohlberg's techniques would then offer themselves as an obvious and useful tool and, moreover, one more likely to succeed than attempts to teach patterns of moral reasoning culled from the pages of the moral philosophers, who are almost inevitably operating at levels which the average pupil, or prisoner, cannot comprehend. But this rationale of Kohlberg's method stands at the opposite extreme from Kohlberg's own. Instead he explicitly rejects the value-neutral approach to moral education precisely because it depends on a value-relativism which he takes his own researches to have disproved. Moral education, for him, should be non-indoctrinative, certainly, but it should also aim at the development of universal, and in that sense objective, values and principles of conduct.

II

Now there are, it seems to me, four ways in which Kohlberg might wish to justify moral development in his sense, i.e. the development of moral reasoning, as a legitimate goal for moral education. First, and most obviously, it might be argued that the development of moral reasoning does after all carry with it an improvement in moral conduct. For an increasing number of studies suggest that there is some connection here, that higher-stage moral reasoners are more likely to do the moral thing, at least as defined by the moral researcher (for a comprehensive survey see Blasi, 1980). But the evidence is scrappy and often conflicting – in the classic study of the Berkeley Free Speech Movement (Haan *et al.*, 1968) Stage 2 thinkers were every bit as likely to join the sit-in as were those at Stage 5, whereas those in between, at Stages 3 and 4, were not; another detailed study (Blatt and Kohlberg, 1975) found that those who moved up a stage were actually more likely to cheat than those who did not – and in any case tend to show only a difference between the minority of Stage 5 and 6 reasoners and the rest, rather than indicating any systematic improvement in conduct as individuals move from one stage to the next.

What we need at this point is some account of the connection between moral thought and action, the most important but also the most complex problem in this whole area, but whatever the precise connection it is worth noting that there are special difficulties for the cognitive-developmental theory in particular (Locke, 1983). There is not just the general problem of how far a person can be relied on to do as he says, or even believes, that he ought, or how far his actions will represent his beliefs. There is also the more specific problem of relating the particular judgement or action to any particular level of moral thinking.

For on the one hand there are allegedly six stages of moral reasoning, but reduced to its simplest only two courses of action available in any concrete situation: either to do it, or not. Hence the particular behaviour can tell us nothing about the level of moral reasoning; one and the same piece of conduct might result from moral thinking at different stages. As against this it might be argued that moral conduct cannot be identified purely behaviourally, that we have to take the agent's reasons into account as well so that what the agent does is in part a matter of the form of reasoning he has used: the Stage 2 protestors, for example, were not strictly doing the same thing as those who sat in for Stage 5 reasons (Broughton, 1978, p. 87). But although this will ensure a one–one correlation between behaviour and level of reasoning, it does so only by making the connection tautological, and hence useless for purposes of prediction and explanation.

On the other hand the various stages of moral reasoning are identified by their form not their content, by the sorts of consideration the individual appeals to in justifying his moral judgements, not the particular judgements that he makes. So reasoning at one and the same level can result in quite different, even conflicting, decisions about what to do and hence, to the extent that thought does determine action, quite different courses of conduct. So even if we did have some general theory of the relationship between thought and action, there would still be no way of inferring someone's conduct from their stage of reasoning, or vice versa: the level of moral reasoning will not even determine what he thinks he ought to do, much less what he actually will do. What this means, it seems to me, is that any adequate account of the relationship between moral thought and moral action will have to take account of its content – particular moral opinions or judgements – as well as the form, or style of reasoning.

So as Kohlberg himself seems well aware in rejecting any behavioural test for the validity of his measures of moral development, it seems there can be no direct connection between level of reasoning and actual conduct. Indeed to the extent that there does seem some correlation between the two, there would also appear to be something amiss with the theory. In particular the connection between the form of moral reasoning and its content – the sorts of reasons you appeal to and the particular judgements you arrive at – seems closer than Kohlberg is inclined to allow. A certain pattern of thinking, e.g. an appeal to the attitudes of the people you know, or to the rules of your community, combined with a certain social setting, some specific set of attitudes or rules, is likely to determine very closely which particular judgements the particular individual ends up with, even if it then remains as problematic as ever whether he will or will not actually act on that judgement.

In fact Kohlberg himself insists that this distinction between form and content breaks down at the final, ultimate stage of moral reasoning, Stage 6: 'our conception of moral principle implies that one cannot ultimately separate form and content in moral analysis' (Kohlberg, 1971b, p. 60). Here, at last, we arrive at a unique and universal set of moral principles – or rather a particular principle, of justice, equality and respect for persons – adequate to resolve all moral problems. And this, in turn, provides us with a second possible justification of moral development as the goal of moral education:

> The problem of offering a non-indoctrinative education which is based on ethical and epistemological principles is partially resolved by a conception that these principles represent developmentally advanced or mature stages of reasoning, judgement and action. Because there are culturally universal stages or sequences in moral development ... stimulation of the child's development to the next step in a natural direction is equivalent to the long range goal of teaching ethical principles. (Kohlberg and Mayer, 1972, p. 475)

Now this claim that there is some universal moral principle, uniquely suited to solving moral difficulties, which everyone will agree on if only they can arrive at Stage 6 is, of course, an extremely bold one, both psychologically and philosophically. I have criticised it in detail elsewhere (Locke, 1980, 1985), but there is perhaps one point that is worth repeating here, concerning the ambiguity of 'universal principle'. This might mean either a principle which is to be applied universally, which is intended to cover everyone, or a principle which is universally adopted, one which everyone accepts. Something like 'Thou shalt not kill' may well be universally adopted, but it is not usually regarded as universally applicable, since we are prepared to exclude killing in self-defence, or in the defence of others, not to mention killing animals and plants. 'Abortion on social grounds is never justified', on the other hand, is meant to be universally applicable, but is certainly not universally accepted. Now clearly, since not everyone reaches Stage 6, the universal principles of Stage 6 will be universal only in the sense of being universally applicable, not in the sense of being universally adopted. But if we fail to notice this difference it is tempting to argue that Stage 6 universal principles must be the same for all those who reach Stage 6: if different people hold different principles, how can they be universal? Thus the ambiguity of 'universal principle' makes it seem that Stage 6 principles must always be the same, whereas – it seems to me – there will always be some disagreement between us over which principles we wish to apply universally, no matter how advanced our moral reasoning.

But even if this is not so, even if there is some ultimate moral principle about which all advanced moral reasoners can agree, it remains arguable whether this provides moral education with a realistic or realisable goal. For in a world where so very few ever get beyond Stage 4 it is, to put it mildly, optimistic, to base moral education on the hope that everyone can eventually be got to Stage 6. Instead it might be more reasonable, and more practicable, to recognise the fact that most individuals remain stuck around Stages 3 and 4, and so concentrate on manipulating the moral environment in such a way that reasoning at these levels will nonetheless lead individuals first to the right opinions, and then to the right actions. Ironically it may well turn out that the just community, a community organised in accordance with Stage 6 principles, might not be the best means of ensuring conduct in accordance with Stage 6 principles! Instead it may fall to those who have reached Stage 6 so to organise society that those at the lower levels of reasoning nevertheless come to do as morality demands: Kohlberg's theories, no less than Skinner's, may yet lead us to the psychological equivalent of Plato's philosopher kings!

There is, however, a third possible justification for Kohlberg's approach to moral education. Instead of appealing to some ultimate goal of attaining universal ethical principles, a goal which seems neither philosophically justifiable nor psychologically attainable, it might be enough that the higher stages of moral reasoning bring with them increasingly more adequate ways of handling moral problems, of resolving and reconciling moral claims and conflicts. It is on this claim, after all, that the claim to derive moral 'oughts' from the facts of human development depend, and if it is correct then, while moral development in this sense might not be the whole of moral education, it would at least be a justifiable part. Yet curiously this is a claim for which Kohlberg nowhere offers much support. Apart from the spurious arguments for Stage 6 which I have criticised elsewhere (Locke, 1980, 1985), there is no attempt to show how the higher stages do resolve problems arising at lower stages, while the empirical evidence actually suggests that subjects move up a stage even when exposed to *conflicting* reasoning at that higher stage (Turiel, 1966), in which case the explanation of the change can hardly be that it enables them to resolve their moral conflicts! In fact, when he considers the details of reasoning at the different stages (1971a, pp. 195–213), Kohlberg is more concerned to show how each stage reveals a growing awareness of the true nature of morality, a more sophisticated understanding of the scope of moral reasoning: a Stage 3 reasoner can look at things from the other person's point of view in a way that a Stage 2 reasoner cannot; a Stage 4 reasoner can see things from the point of view of the community as a whole, not just particular individuals; and so on. Yet as Kohlberg himself seems aware (1971a, p. 182), this improvement in an individual's understanding of the nature of morality and moral reasoning is not at all the same thing as an increased ability to solve moral problems. Once again it may well prove the reverse: the more sophisticated our moral understanding, the more difficult it may be to resolve conflicting moral claims. Certainly someone resting secure in the ethical egoism of Stage 2 may find it easier to decide what to do, than someone agonising over individual rights and social utilities at Stage 5!

This brings us finally to a fourth, and more modest, justification of moral development as a goal of moral education. If the movement from stage to stage does not guarantee any improvement in moral conduct, nor bring us any closer to universally acceptable moral principles, nor increase our ability to resolve and reconcile moral claims and conflicts, at least it does seem to involve a growing understanding of what morality is and what it involves, and therefore not only of what constitutes a moral problem, but also of what would constitute an adequate solution. It is in this, I suspect, that the greater cognitive adequacy of the higher stages consists, although so far from making it easier to solve moral problems this heightened moral awareness should actually make it more difficult. Nevertheless if what we are looking for is not moral solutions but moral understanding, an improvement in the level of moral reasoning may give us what we want. To the extent that moral education should be concerned not with improving people's conduct, nor with inculcating moral principles, nor with merely improving the level of reasoning as such, but with improving people's recognition of when they have a moral problem, and of what they should take into account in trying to resolve that problem, then to that extent moral development, in Kohlberg's sense, might indeed constitute a justifiable and appropriate goal for moral education. It may be less than Kohlberg himself had hoped for. But it may be enough.

III

So far I have been concerned with what might be called the 'orthodox' Kohlbergian theory of moral education, as developed in a series of authoritative essays in the early 1970s (Kohlberg, 1971b; Kohlberg and Mayer, 1972; Kohlberg and Turiel, 1971). By the end of the decade, however, personal experience had led Kohlberg to change his mind on a number of key issues, in ways which in effect concede the points which I have been making. Since these essays (Kohlberg, 1978, 1980) may be less well known, or less easily available, I shall quote from them at more length.

The most striking change is that Kohlberg now insists that moral education both must and should be indoctrinative, precisely because moral education must concern itself with the content of moral thought as well as with its form or structure, and with behaviour as well as thinking:

> The psychologist's abstract concept 'moral stage' is not a sufficient basis for moral education. Abstracting moral 'cognition' (judg-

ment and reasoning) from moral action and abstracting structure in moral cognition and judgment from content are necessary for certain psychological research purposes. Although the moral stage concept is valuable for research purposes, however, it is not a sufficient guide to the moral educator, who deals with concrete morality in a school world in which value content as well as structure, behaviour as well as reasoning, must be dealt with. In this context the educator must be a socializer, teaching value content and behaviour, not merely a Socratic facilitator of development. In becoming a socializer and advocate, the teacher moves into 'indoctrination' ... I now believe that the concepts guiding moral education must be partly 'indoctrinative' (1978, p. 84)

This amounts to conceding my first point: if moral education is to affect behaviour as well as thought – and surely it should – then at the very least it will have to influence the content of moral thinking, as well as its form; it will have to ensure that people have the right moral beliefs, before they can begin to act on them. Admittedly, even that may not be enough to ensure that people do behave morally, but it does seem a necessary starting point.

Kohlberg has also abandoned any hope – if, indeed, he ever had it – that a moral education based on moral development might increase the number of Stage 6 moral reasoners, and thereby facilitate the spread of Stage 6 moral principles. On this point he now sounds decidedly pessimistic, tracing a gradual decline in the general level of public moral aspiration, and a corresponding decline in the achievable goals of moral education. At least in the 1960s, the era of campus agitation over civil, and student, rights and the Vietnam war, 'the quest for justice and a concern for what I called the sixth stage of universal principles moved in the land' (1980, p. 456). By the mid-1970s, post-Watergate, however, the dominant concern had moved back to 'the vision of Jefferson and the founding fathers I called Stage 5 ... the morality of social contract and the rights of man which generated the Declaration of Independence and the Constitution' (p. 456). And by the end of the decade it was proving difficult enough to encourage or develop moral, social and political thinking even at Stage 4:

> In the sixties, we seemed to see youth groping toward principled fifth or even sixth stage reasoning, and recoiling from fourth stage

political leadership while being misunderstood as immoral and lawless. Today the misunderstanding is a stage down. The youth groping toward some fourth stage conception of a political community are alienated at the personal and institutional or collective egoism of institutional leadership (p. 463).

According Kohlberg now advocates 'further retrenchment to Stage 4 goals as the ends of civic education' (1980, p. 459), goals which he had previously rejected for 'teaching respect for law and order, authority, nation, and the free enterprise system on the value side, and straight facts on the cognitive side' (p. 458). But the goal now is 'not attainment of the fifth stage, but a solid attainment of the fourth stage commitment to being a good member of a community or a good citizen' (p. 459). What is required, in other words, is not Stage 4 reasoning as such, but a particular, acceptable, set of Stage 4 values, a particular Stage 4 content. The justification for this retrenchment, moreover, is not, as I suggested it might be, that Stage 4 provides a cognitively, and therefore morally, superior mode of moral thinking to the even more common lower stages, nor that it involves an increased moral awareness or insight. The justification is simply Kohlberg's concern, or despair, at the increased public and political prominence of Stage 2, 'look out for number one', reasoning, as expressed, for example, in what he terms the 'new conservatism'. The grounds on which he favours this new goal of moral education, in other words, are neither psychological nor philosophical. They are purely moral, even ideological.

What we have, then, is no longer moral development as the goal of moral education. Instead it is – of all things – socialisation which provides both the goal and a technique for moral education. To repeat, this new

> approach is not merely Socratic and developmental, it is indoctrinative ... Its philosophy of civic education is in a certain sense ... conventional or fourth stage. Only its educational approach is unconventional and new. The approach is the governance of a small community by participatory or direct democracy. Rules are made and enforced through a community meeting, one-person-one-vote whether faculty or student. (1980, p. 459)

Yet even this has proved doubtfully effective: in the very case described by Kohlberg, 'moral and positive attitudes of participation in the democratic school ... have not transferred to the larger civic world, in the absence of a parallel process of participation in the broader community' (p. 469). With moral development as the goal of moral education there was the hope that we might change society by changing, by morally educating, individuals. But if a form of socialisation – we might call it democratic socialisation – is now the aim, it seems that we can change individuals only by changing society. What we seem to need, in other words, is not moral education but social change. And 'just community' experiments, in schools or in prisons, will not provide us with that.

What was most exciting about Kohlberg's theory of moral development, I suggested, was the way in which it straddled, and combined, the three disciplines of psychology, philosophy and education. What was original in his theory of moral education, I suggested, was the way in which it provided a solid theoretical rationale for an approach, based on open democratic classroom discussion and decision-making, which was hardly original to Kohlberg and his associates. But the theoretical rationale seemed inadequate, and has therefore collapsed, separating the practice of moral education from the philosophy and psychology of moral development. Kohlberg's moral educational aim of good citizenship may be acceptable enough – I certainly would not want to quarrel with *that!* – but it is both more conventional and less original than it originally seemed to be.

REFERENCES

Blasi, A., 'Bridging Moral Cognition and Moral Action: a Critical Review of the Literature', *Psychological Bulletin*, 1980, vol. 88, 1–45.

Blatt, M. and Kohlberg, L., 'The Effects of Classroom Discussion Upon Children's Level of Moral Judgment', *Journal of Moral Education*, 1975, vol. 4, 129–61.

Broughton, J., 'The Cognitive-Developmental Approach to Morality: a Reply to Kurtines and Greif', *Journal of Moral Education*, 1978, vol. 7, 81–96.

Haan, N., Smith, M. B. and Block, J., 'Moral Reasoning of Young Adults: Political–Social Behaviour, Family Background, and Personality Correlates', *Journal of Personality and Social Psychology*, 1968, vol. 10, 183–201.

Kohlberg, L., 'Stage and Sequence: the Cognitive-Developmental Approach to Socialization', in D. Goslin (ed.), *Handbook of Socialization Theory and Research* (Chicago: Rand McNally, 1969).

——, 'From Is To Ought: How to Commit the Naturalistic Fallacy and Get Away with It in the Study of Moral Development', in T. Mischel (ed.),

Cognitive Development and Epistemology (New York: Academic Press, 1971(a)).
——, 'Stages of Moral Development as a Basis for Moral Education' in C. M. Beck, B. S. Crittenden and E. V. Sullivan (eds), *Moral Education: Interdisciplinary Approaches* (University of Toronto Press, 1971(b) 23–92.
——, 'Moral Stages and Moralization' in T. Lickona (ed.), *Moral Development and Behaviour: Theory, Research and Social Issues* (New York: Holt, Rinehart & Winston, 1976).
——, 'Revisions in the Theory and Practice of Moral Development' in W. Damon (ed.), *Moral Development (New Directions for Child Development*, 2), (San Francisco: Jossey Bass, 1978).
——, 'Educating for a Just Society: an Updated and Revised Statement' in B. Munsey (ed.), *Moral Development, Moral Education, and Kohlberg* (Birmingham, Alabama: Religious Education Press, 1980).
Kohlberg, L., Kauffman, K., Scharf, P. and Hickey, J., 'The Just Community Approach to Corrections: a theory' *Journal of Moral Education*, 1975, vol. 4, 243–60.
Kohlberg, L. and Mayer, R., 'Development as the Aim of Education', *Harvard Educational Review*, 1972, vol. 42, 449–96.
Kohlberg, L. and Turiel, E., 'Moral Development and Moral Education' in C. Beck and E. Sullivan (eds), *Psychology and Educational Practice* (Glenview, Ill.: Scott Foresman, 1971).
Locke, D., 'Cognitive Stages or Development Phases?: a Critique of Kohlberg's Stage Structural Theory of Moral Reasoning', *Journal of Moral Education*, 1979, vol. 8, 168–81.
——, 'The Illusion of Stage Six, *Journal of Moral Education*, 1980, vol. 9, 103–10.
——, 'Doing What Comes Morally: the Relation between Behaviour and Stages of Moral Reasoning, *Human Development*, 1983, vol. 26, 11–25.
——, 'A Psychologist Among the Philosophers: Philosophical Aspects of Kohlberg's Theories' in S. and C. Modgil (eds), *Lawrence Kohlberg: Consensus and Controversy* (Lewes: Falmer Press, 1985).
Turiel, E., 'An Experimental Test of the Sequentiality of Developmental Stage in the Child's Moral Judgments', *Journal of Personality and Social Psychology*, 1966, vol. 3, 611–18.

10 The Roots of Moral Reason

RENFORD BAMBROUGH

Is there a supreme arithmetical principle? Or a supreme principle of physics or economics or law or history? Is it even possible that there should be a supreme principle of any of these branches of knowledge or enquiry? If not, is the lack of such a principle fatal to the pretensions of any of these studies to be called a branch of knowledge?

These questions about each of these enquiries may be summed up in two questions: Is a supreme principle in each or any of these cases *possible*? And is a supreme principle in each or any of these cases *necessary*? Professor Alan Gewirth believes that a supreme principle of morality is both necessary and possible. In *Reason and Morality*[1] he sets out arguments for these two beliefs, and also for the Principle of Generic Consistency which is, according to him, the supreme principle of which morality stands in need and with which it may be furnished. My own belief is that a supreme principle of morality is neither necessary nor possible.

By speaking first of non-moral enquiries I have hinted at one part of my argument against Gewirth. Comparisons between moral philosophy and the philosophy of mathematics and physics and law and history soon reveal that there is serious unclarity about the *question* whether there is or can be or must be a supreme moral principle. We do not know how to answer or how to begin to answer the questions raised in my opening paragraph. The corresponding question about morality is at least as unclear as those questions about history and science and mathematics, but many philosophers have persuaded themselves that it is a clear question, and have proceeded to defend and criticise rival answers to it.

In questioning the question I am involving myself in general

philosophy as well as moral philosophy. This unclarity about principles, their grounds and their sources, their necessity and possibility, is
the cause of perpetual controversy in metaphysics and epistemology.
We cannot deal adequately with Gewirth's question about morality
by dealing generally with the problem of the foundations of knowledge and treating the problem of the foundations of moral knowledge as just another particular case. It is a *different* case, raising
issues of its own that cannot be resolved by resolving the general
problem of foundations. The difference is one of the main themes of
Moral Scepticism and Moral Knowledge.[2] But the more general
problem is the main issue between Gewirth and myself,[3] and is also a
central theme in the philosophy of education, including the philosophy of moral education.

Gewirth believes that a supreme principle is possible because he
believes that it is necessary. He knows the nature and force of the
objections to the idea of a supreme principle, and he sets them out
persuasively (pp. 7ff.). But he believes both that it is possible to justify
moral conclusions and that justification must take the form of a
pyramid with a supreme principle as its apex, and therefore that a
supreme principle is possible. (His principle is like Plato's Form of
the Good: it is a dimensionless apex and yet infinitely rich in
content).

Gewirth suspects 'some contemporary philosophers' (p. 8) including myself (note 4, p. 368) of accepting current moral judgements and
standards just because they are there:

> Just as the older intuitionists hold that one can see by direct
> intellectual inspection what ought to be done in each morally
> relevant situation, so some contemporary philosophers have held
> it to be self-evident that, for example, wantonly inflicting pain
> upon another person is always at least prima facie morally wrong.
> Similar self-evidence has been held to attach to the obligations to
> keep one's promises and to tell the truth. Since we know such
> moral propositions, there is no need to justify them; hence too, a
> fortiori, there is no need to justify a supreme moral principle as the
> ground or justificans for justifying particular moral propositions or
> general rules.

The footnote cites my paper 'A Proof of the Objectivity of Morals'
(*American Journal of Jurisprudence* 14 (1969)), together with G. J.
Warnock's book *The Object of Morality* and papers by William H.

Gass, J. R. Lucas and R. F. Holland. My article has now been revised and extended into chapter II of *Moral Scepticism and Moral Knowledge*. If Gewirth had been able to read the book rather than just an early version of one of its chapters, I do not think he could plausibly have classed me as a kind of intuitionist, even if (as I doubt) the article as it stood in 1969 gave colour to the charge.

He thinks that my approach involves me in abandoning all hope of justification, in declaring that though justification is not possible it is also not necessary. But it is a supreme principle that I declare to be neither possible nor necessary. I believe that justification is necessary and that it is possible. It does not take the form of an appeal to a hierarchy or pyramid of principles. The foundations picture that holds Gewirth captive is not the only or the best picture. Moral reason is not an edifice built upon a rock, but a tree fed and watered by its roots.

This alternative and better picture has been painted by an author to whom Gewirth surprisingly never refers. In his *Values and Imperatives*[4] C. I. Lewis has a chapter entitled 'Pragmatism and the Roots of the Moral' and says that its topic 'concerns the roots of the moral sense and the fundamental principles of ethics' (p. 103). The merits of this metaphor are more fully expounded by John Stuart Mill in the first chapter of *Utilitarianism*:

> The truths which are ultimately accepted as the first principles of a science, are really the last results of metaphysical analysis, practised on the elementary notions with which the science is conversant; and their relation to the science is not that of foundations to an edifice, but of roots to a tree, which may perform their office equally well though they be never dug down to and exposed to light.

Lewis speaks of 'the roots of the moral' in his chapter heading but in the first paragraph of the chapter he speaks of the roots of the moral *sense*. I have changed to the roots of moral *reason* because talk of a moral sense too easily reminds people of what they regard as superstitious and unhealthy notions of intuition, or encourages them to think of morality as all feeling and no thinking.

Reason, even in the singular, is also less likely to lend itself to the oversimplification and excessive tidiness that Prichard complains of.[5] The senses would have to be plural and numerous to cover the actualities of moral experience and moral debate.

The absurdity of requiring a single supreme principle as the foundation and justification of morality is evoked by asking whether the inculcation of such a principle could be the usual way, or any way at all, of initiating a child into the understanding of good and evil, right and wrong. A child learns when to say 'It's not fair' or 'Thank you' or 'I couldn't help it' before meeting any conceivable candidate for the role of supreme principle, as a child learns to count from one to twenty and to multiply by three or seventeen before being introduced to any candidates for the role of foundations or axioms of arithmetic.[6]

No explanation of facts or concepts of economics could be given to a person who had no observation or experience of buying and selling, exchange and barter. In giving such explanations it is necessary to rely on an appeal to what a person already knows in being familiar with these operations.

Morality, like arithmetic and commerce, is a *going concern*. We find ourselves involved in it, as we find ourselves on Emerson's staircase, before it can occur to us to ask where it comes from or where it may end: 'Where do we find ourselves? In a series, of which we do not know the extremes, and believe that it has none. We wake, and find ourselves on a stair: there are stairs below us, which we seem to have ascended; there are stairs above us, many a one, which go upward and out of sight.'[7]

The philosophical problems about morality arise from difficulties that we meet within morality, just as philosophical problems about knowledge in general arise from difficulties that present themselves within non-philosophical enquiries. Prichard pays attention to this parallel. This was to be expected of a philosopher who saw as clearly as Prichard did that both morality and enquiry generally are going concerns. We start in the midst of things. It is not just that we cannot do philosophy until we are able to conduct non-philosophical enquiries, but that in all enquiries, philosophical or non-philosophical, we find ourselves, even at our initiation, engaged in an enterprise which has no identifiable beginning. Emerson accordingly speaks of our finding ourselves on the staircase and seeing that the stairs go upwards and downwards without ending.

Prichard is faithful to his insight into morality as a going concern when he warns us not to expect simplicity or tidiness in our moral conceptions. For all we know, he says, our moral obligations may form 'an unrelated chaos'. He accordingly rejects attempts to impose unity or simplicity by seeking a principle or definition from which moral truths can be derived as consequences. This in turn sets him against two familiar species of moral philosophers: those who try to *justify* moral conclusions by such a derivation, and those who seek only to *articulate* in a tidy *criterion* (Prichard's own word, p. 14) the deliverances of some other source of moral enlightenment.

Yet Prichard has not altogether abandoned the foundationist picture of moral and general knowledge, even though he has rejected its most intolerable consequences. His concept of intuition is the last resort of a thinker who has rejected the standard answers to the questions 'How do we know...?' and 'What is our criterion ...?', without altogether rejecting the questions. He has nowhere else to turn while he remains loyal to the foundations picture. Things look different when we come to dig down to the roots.

We shall not be able to find the roots if we forget the fruit and the flowers. Digging down to the roots is at the same time exploring the gardens and fields, thickets and jungles, in which human life is lived. In moral epistemology as in general epistemology we can be helped by giving ourselves the *description* that Wittgenstein asked for and provided. In both cases, too, the description gives us a better understanding, and therefore deserves to be counted as a species of explanation, in spite of Wittgenstein's own insistence that description is to be contrasted with explanation and offered instead of it.

The roots of reason in general are found by Wittgenstein in 'something animal', in the life that human animals live together.[8] Peirce gives a parallel account when he traces the human understanding to our instincts as animal creatures.[9] Both are engaged in investigating what Wittgenstein explicitly calls the 'natural history' of the human species. In this respect they are reminiscent of the eighteenth century empiricists who undertook to introduce observational methods into 'moral subjects', who wrote enquiries, essays and treatises on the human understanding and human nature, and did not, like the philosophers of today, fear that a corrupting 'psychologism' would invalidate any acount of knowledge and reason that took the form of a description of the powers of the mind.

There is no such inhibition against finding the roots of morality in 'the fabric and constitution of the human species' (Hume), but most of those who follow this path do not regard themselves as uncovering the roots of moral reason. They typically think of morality as unreasoned, as rooted in irrational feelings or non-rational attitudes. Peirce and Wittgenstein, by displaying the rootedness of all our reasonings in our human fabric and constitution, remove a stubborn obstacle to the right understanding of morality.

Peirce, again like Wittgenstein, associates his naturalist picture of human knowledge with a repudiation of the search for a Cartesian bedrock. You cannot start by doubting everything, for you are already, when you start, 'laden with an immense mass of cognition already formed, of which you cannot divest yourself if you would; and who knows whether, if you could, you would not have made all knowledge impossible to yourself?'[10] We are on the staircase, but we have no memory or record of a first step.

Even when we become conscious of our involvement in the going concerns of theoretical and practical enquiry and deliberation, we still have no choice about the fact of our involvement. This is brought out by attending to the parallel between Peirce's treatment of Doubt, Surprise, Experience and Belief and a treatment of Indignation, Resentment and Guilt towards which Strawson in 'Freedom and Resentment' offers a valuable contribution.[11] The two groups of concepts have in common, in spite of the differences between their respective environments of the True and the Good, two features that are keys to their indispensable roles in epistemology and moral epistemology:

(1) They come to us unchosen and unbidden: we do not *decide* to be surprised or resentful, baffled or ashamed.
(2) Yet surprise and bafflement, shame and resentment are not describable or intelligible except as *assessments*, as *evaluations* of that to which we are responding when we feel surprised, ashamed, baffled or resentful.

The parallel extends to the nature of the procedures that take their starting points from these states of mind. If I am startled or shocked, astonished or indignant, I may appropriately reflect on whether it is appropriate that I should feel or express such a response. Reflection on a doubt may lead to a change in a belief. Indignation or a response to indignation may provoke a reconsideration that ends in apology. Or the belief or doubt or condemnation may stand at the end of the process of reflection where it stood at the beginning. What cannot happen is that I should understand and endorse the terms in which such assessments, whether logical, causal or moral, are expressed and conducted, and yet renounce, or just lose, all commitment to all such propositional or practical attitudes as belief, surprise, reproach or indignation.

Aristotle's recognition that deliberation is about means and not about ends is a consequence of his understanding that these attitudes and responses form a network, like the 'system' that Wittgenstein outlines in *On Certainty*, from which our practical questions derive their meaning.[12] I cannot be starting from scratch when wondering what to do or what to praise or prize any more than in wondering what to believe or how to argue. The understanding of a question, theoretical or practical, brings with it the understanding of the relevance of certain considerations whose relevance is accordingly recognised by conflicting parties to any dispute about the question. Otherwise it would not be the same question that they were disputing about, but two or more different questions concerning which they were at cross-purposes.

Even within the present brief compass it is possible and advisable to look at a few cases of actual moral perplexity or conflict to illustrate and underwrite my main conclusions.

(1) Why do we punish a successful criminal more severely than one who is equally culpable but who through accident or incompetence fails to commit his robbery or murder?

(2) The Roman Catholic priest of an English parish has been found guilty of participating in an IRA bombing. He wishes to return to his parish after serving his sentence, but some of his flock ask for a change of shepherd. What should the Bishop do?

(3) Is it reasonable to hold a twentieth century European or American responsible for acts of aggression or oppression committed by his ancestors in earlier centuries?

(4) Why does the Geneva Convention provide that prisoners of war who are released while hostilities continue shall not return to the fighting?

(5) Why were the Marines who had been overwhelmed by the Argentine invasion of the Falkland Islands keen to join the Task Force sent to recover the Islands? Is question (5) connected with question (4)?

(6) Why should a crime committed by one member of a family be thought to bring disgrace on the family?

(7) A man is driving a car when it collides with a pedestrian, who is killed. The police, the coroner and the family of the dead woman are all insistent that he is in no way to blame. He continues to say that he feels guilty. Is he being irrational?

Five brief comments must serve to adumbrate how we might come to grips with these seven issues.

(a) There are utilitarian reasons for being more severe on a successful attempt. For example, a man trying to escape from the police after an unsuccessful attempt at murder is more likely to make further attempts if his sentence upon conviction cannot be increased by them. But there is more to it than that. We *care* more if actual harm is done than if it is not, and the greater the harm the more we care.

(b) It is natural to feel something that it is natural to call guilt if we are agents, however innocent, of bringing harm to others. We should probably tie down 'guilt' in such a way that the man *is* irrational if he feels *guilt* when he is as innocent as he is in my example. But the driver's reaction is *appropriately* different from that of any person not involved so directly in the story of the death. It is not a matter of physical proximity: I may be in the passenger seat beside him, and not feel as he feels, even though, like him, I am shaken and shocked as a mere eyewitness could not be, still less a newspaper reader learning of it all from the inquest report.

The feeling is one that finds expression in the ancient Athenians' practice of requiring ritual purification of one who, however innocently, caused the death of another human being. If we call this feeling a sense of 'pollution' we are more likely to feel, as A. W. H. Adkins does, that it is irrational.[13] But the friend of mine on whose experience I base this example did feel *tainted* by the death in which he was implicated, even when he knew that his involvement was wholly innocent.

(c) The bomber-priest will be a less successful shepherd of a flock containing members who regard him as a murderer, even if (perhaps especially if) if contains others who regard him as a hero. There is also the feeling that a priest should be an example to us, and not an example of evil-doing. A man with blood on his hands should not be in the holy places, bury the dead, baptise the infants.

(d) My kinship with my ancestors and my descendants, or with my fellow-countrymen, like my closer kinship with my parents and my children, makes it natural – *understandable* – that I should feel shame at their misdeeds, pride in their achievements, grief at their loss, joy in their happiness. The idea of taint or dishonour here again finds fertile soil.

(e) If released prisoners could return to the fighting they would never be released. Besides this practical point there is the fact that prisoners who are smarting under the fact, and perhaps the nature, of their captivity, may be feeling too vengeful to abide by the proper constraints of civilised warfare. It was argued on analogous grounds that the Marines driven from the Falklands should not have returned there until the islands were recaptured and at peace, even though a formal state of war did not exist.

We find recurring in these examples reactions and responses of the kind described by Strawson, and we find one such reaction linked with others in networks whose full tracing out would be a full description of the life of human beings.

These reactions and responses are so prominent in any account of how we actually discuss our moral problems that we must characterise their role correctly if we are not to fall into confusion about the whole subject. We need first to distinguish their relevance as *data for* moral assessments and their role as *constituents of* moral assessments. The fact that victims of crime tend to seek or desire revenge is a fact about human beings that our arrangements for the administration of justice need to provide for. The fact that Aunt Felicity will be disappointed and resentful if her annual visit is postponed or cancelled is a fact to be taken into account in deciding whether to take that sudden and attractive opportunity for a holiday in Greece. But the concern for Aunt Felicity that is expressed in our deliberation and discussion of the question is constitutive of the moral agency of those who have to decide the matter. And in the larger field of crime and punishment we have not exhausted the relevance of human reactions when we have treated them as the material of which the situations of human life are made. They are also the forms in which our recognition of values is embodied. The distinction is illustrated by Bacon's remark, too pregnant to be easy to understand, that revenge is a kind of wild justice. He need not mean that it is a kind of *ferocious* justice, but rather that it is the forest or jungle plant whose domesticated and cultivated form grows to maturity in any community that deserves to be called a civil society.

It is no wonder that an inexplicit and incomplete recognition of the *formal* role of these reactions should express itself in subjectivist and relativist accounts of the relation of moral thinking and feeling. Am I not admitting that a moral judgement is or involves, as Hume and his successors have always said, the expression of an emotional attitude towards its object? Yes, I admit this and insist upon it, just as I admit and insist that a non-moral judgement is or involves one of those reactions that Peirce and Wittgenstein describe and discuss, such as doubt or hope or surprise or confidence. Is *all* knowledge subjective or relative?

A reaction or response, moral or non-moral, is the response of a subject. To describe it is to describe the *person* whose reaction it is. But the person whom we characterise as doubtful, surprised or confident is doubtful *whether* the bridge will bear the weight, surprised or confident *that* the flood is subsiding. His reaction is at the same time an *assessment*, and the assessment is sound or unsound, well or ill based. It is either true or false that the bridge will collapse, that the flood level is steady or still rising. Whether it is true or false that things are as the reacting subject takes them to be, it is also true or false that he is right or reasonable to take them to be as he takes them to be.

In deciding whether things *are* as he takes them to be, and whether it is reasonable for him to take them to be as he takes them to be, we rely on our existing knowledge and understanding of how things are. If we discuss either of these questions with him, we rely on his and our shared knowledge of how things are. There is no possibility of enquiry or deliberation or discussion or disagreement without reference to what is, in advance of such enquiry or deliberation, known or understood. This is what makes scepticism so plausible, since the sceptic can insistently ask how we know or understand the things on which we rely when we are debating or discussing the immediate point at issue between us. What is q founded on even if p *is* founded on q?

Here again a change of picture is needed. The linear pattern that goes with the foundations metaphor needs to be exchanged for the image of a *network*, which better expresses the relations between the manifold elements in the system of our knowledge and understanding. Through this picture we can express the main features of our concepts of reason and justification in a way that reconciles what on the linear and foundationist view seem to be incompatible requirements:

(1) There is no end to any process of justification.
(2) It is possible to justify a conclusion.

When establishing a conclusion to our own satisfaction, or supporting a conclusion against the criticism of others, we do not often need to attend to anything *fundamental* or *radical*, i.e. to anything which, in whichever of these two metaphorical forms we choose to express it, is regarded as part of the background against which our ordinary questions arise and are settled. When such a need does arise, as it necessarily does in philosophy, and may at any time arise within physics, law, history etc., the appeal that we then make to what is *more deeply rooted* in our knowledge and understanding is at the same time an appeal to what is more *elementary*; and that is another way of saying what we said earlier, that the ultimate appeal is to the *teaching*. Since the teaching is not the inculcation of a principle or of a small set of axioms, the appeal to it is not an appeal to such a principle or to such axioms. It is rather to a practice that all parties to the conflict have adopted in the very process of acquiring understanding that is necessary even for grasping that a question is at issue, and understanding *what* question is at issue.

What I have been saying about justification and deliberation goes for innovation and reform too. Gewirth shares the suspicion of many critics that my account of reason and argument leaves no scope for change in thought and society, but grips us in a deadening conservatism from which it necessarily debars any possible escape. Once again the reply is to compare moral reason with reason outside the sphere of morals. A scientific revolution, a philosophical revolution, a political revolution, if it is more than just a *change*, is grounded in something permanent or more permanent in the very tradition against which it is reacting. This is the large scale application of what on the smaller scale of individual thought comes to this: that in every sphere of enquiry the learner may come to question what he has been taught, but when he does so he is appealing *to* what he has been taught as well as *against* what he has been taught.

All this applies even to the debate about and between the metaphors of roots and foundations, i.e. to the debate between Gewirth and myself and to all debates about the foundations of knowledge, the project of pure enquiry, the limits of knowledge, the search for an answer to scepticism. This is usefully illustrated by two features of Gewirth's own work.

The first of the two features has been diagnosed and well treated by Marcus Singer, and I need not enlarge upon it here.[14] It is the use that Gewirth makes of what used to be called the deliverances of the ordinary moral consciousness. As Singer says (pp. 27–8), Gewirth relies on standard normative assumptions and is prepared to do a bit of tinkering with his machinery to produce what we all know to be the right moral result (pp. 33 and 36). Singer might well have noted here, as I had noted before I knew that this subject had been justly dealt with by Singer, that Gewirth's treatment of abortion (pp. 142–4) is a striking instance of the same phenomenon. My references to Prichard on tidiness and chaos will have shown already how sympathetic I am to Singer's complaints against Gewirth's ethical monism.

The second feature is found in the citadel of Gewirth's whole structure, since it concerns his use of the notion of a rational agent. His use of it involves a more fundamental but still implicit reliance than Singer and I have so far noted on our ordinary patterns of moral thinking and moral practice. He can persuade himself that he is deriving all his detailed results *from* his supreme principle only because they are summed up *in* the principle. What is summed up in the apex of his pyramid needs to be unpacked and laid out if we are to see what is supporting what. Gewirth himself does lay it out, and in doing so he uses one effective method of drawing attention to the elementary facts about reasoning and enquiry (practical as well as theoretical) to which I am appealing when I speak of both modes of reasoning as *going concerns*. He could not frame his notion of a rational agent without relying on the rich knowledge of agents and their circumstances that we all share, and some of which is illustrated in my examples of moral problems and our means of resolving them. Gewirth regards his principle as a narrow starting point for a programme of justification. I regard it as a broad summation of the results of the enterprise of description that is basic to the needs of the philosophy of morals. Gewirth's agent is recognisably a human being, and every agent must be a human being, or something more than a human being, or not much less than a human being. Gewirth implicitly recognises this: since he wants to get so much out of the concept of an agent, he has to acknowledge that it has a great deal in it. My disagreement with him is about how it came to be there and about what is achieved by first packing it in and then spreading it out.

Here again we can be helped by attending to the parallels between moral philosophy and the philosophy of other branches of human knowledge. When Russell and Whitehead seek the foundations of mathematics they are not seeking to justify or to question the procedures or results of mathematicians or accountants or surveyors. Anything that purports to overturn or impugn our recognition that $7 \times 7 = 49$ or that the square on the hypotenuse of a right-angled triangle is equal to the sum of the squares on the adjacent sides would merely discredit itself by *reductio ad absurdum*.

Similar considerations apply to formulations by logicians of patterns of argument and inference in any field: syllogism; deontic logic; definition of the uses of ordinary words, as sought by Socrates; formulation of rules of language, as sought by Chomsky or by a schoolroom grammarian. In all these cases what is sought is a summary articulation of the structure of a practice. The detailed character of the practice, examined with care, is the test for the accuracy of the articulation.

Russell and others, when engaged in the search for such an articulation, sometimes mislead themselves into speaking as if they were testing the soundness of the foundations of the practice.

The pragmatism of Peirce and Wittgenstein and C. I. Lewis is my base for this critique of Gewirth's foundationism. Their emphasis on the primacy of the particular is at the same time an emphasis on the primacy of practice. Reasoning syllogistically is a going concern before Aristotle codifies its practice. Reasoning deontically is a going concern before twentieth century logicians state or misstate its principles.

Gewirth suspects that we pragmatists and particularists are content to endorse familiar modes of argument simply because they are familiar. He is so attached to this conception of a justification that he does not recognise *as* a justification the only justification that can in the end be offered for a procedure or conclusion of physics or logic, mathematics or morals.

When we question somebody's reasoning we appeal against his practice to *the* practice which is also *his* practice. Socrates confutes Polus or Theaetetus by pointing out something that *he* recognises to be so, and recognises to be so only if what he said at first is *not* so.

This is what happens when we are engaged in moral debate. A student who questions whether the accident of birth confers on him any obligation to be loyal to a nation or government may be asked whether the accident of birth brings with it any obligation to be loyal to his parents.

This is what happens when we are engaged in philosophical debate about morals. One who questions moral objectivism because he thinks it is logically linked with tyranny and inquisition may be asked whether tyranny and inquisition are *only subjectively* objectionable.

This is what is happening when I ask Gewirth whether there is a supreme arithmetical principle, or a supreme principle of physics or economics or law or history, and whether, if not, the lack of such a principle is fatal to the pretensions of any of these studies to be called a branch of knowledge.

NOTES

1. Alan Gewirth, *Reason and Morality* (University of Chicago Press, 1978).
2. Renford Bambrough, *Moral Scepticism and Moral Knowledge* (London: Routledge & Kegan Paul, 1979).
3. The present chapter was originally published in Edward Regis Jr. (ed.), *Gewirth's Ethical Rationalism: Critical Essays with a Reply by Alan Gewirth* (University of Chicago Press, 1984). It is reprinted here by kind permission of the editor and the publisher.
4. Clarence Irving Lewis, *Values and Imperatives: Studies in Ethics* (Stanford University Press, 1969).
5. H. A. Prichard, 'Does Moral Philosophy Rest on a Mistake?', in *Moral Obligation* (Oxford: Clarendon Press, 1949).
6. It has been pointed out to me by several readers that my argument has a close and critical bearing on the work of Lawrence Kohlberg. See his 'Moral Stages and Moralization' in T. Lickona (ed.), *Moral Development and Moral Behaviour* (New York: Holt, Rinehart & Wilson, 1976).
7. Ralph Waldo Emerson, 'Experience', in *Essays* (London: J. M. Dent and Sons; New York: E. P. Dutton & Co. Inc., 1906).
8. L. Wittgenstein, *On Certainty* (Oxford: Basil Blackwell, 1969), s. 359.
9. C. S. Peirce, *Collected Papers* (Cambridge, Mass: Harvard University Press, 1931–5 and 1959) vol. v, s. 173.
10. Peirce, op. cit., vol. v, s. 416.
11. P. F. Strawson, 'Freedom and Resentment', in *Freedom and Resentment and other Essays* (London: Methuen, 1974).
12. Wittgenstein, op. cit., s. 559.
13. A. W. H. Adkins, *Merit and Responsibility: A Study in Greek Values* (Oxford: Clarendon Press, 1960) pp. 91 ff.
14. Marcus G. Singer, 'Gewirth's Ethical Monism' in Regis, op. cit., note 3.

Index